FINDING LOVE GOD'S WAY

ERLITA SUAREZ CABAL

Kiwi Graphix Publishing
New Zealand

Copyright © 2015 Erlita Suarez Cabal and Brendan Roberts
All rights reserved

Published by Kiwi Graphix

ISBN 9781512169355

Cover design © Michelle Dineros

Worth the Chase: Unless otherwise noted Scripture is quoted from the Good News Bible.

Worth Chasing: Unless otherwise noted Scripture is quoted from the New Revised Standard Version Bible.
Printed 2015

Dedication

To God, you're the best writer ever! You're an awesome encourager and mentor! Thank you Father God for the gift and passion for writing you placed in my heart. Thank you for your wisdom and your heart. This is a masterpiece written by you through love and for love.

Papa Virgilio, Mama Gloria, Ate Maribel, Ondoy Geralvin, Mariel, Kuya Jr, Analyn, Ashly Joy, and Boro, I wrote this book out of my love for you all. No words can describe how grateful I am for life's greatest blessing called FAMILY.

Brendan Roberts, words are not enough to express how grateful I am for having you as my bestie, mentor, running mate and prayer buddy.

Michelle Dineros and Hersie Manuel, your constant prayer and encouragement lifts up my spirit. You ladies are awesome! I love you my sisters to the moon and back!

My big little brother Brandon O'Donnell, thank you for always reminding me how beautiful and awesome I am at times when all I could see is my stubborn self.

Ma'am Sydel Uy, thank you for being proud of me. You're one of my best teachers!

Roushiaben Francisco, thank you for pushing me out of my comfort zone. You're an angel!

Aileen Mabilangan and DGROUP sisters, I am forever grateful for our God-centered friendship.

To my Feast Ortigas family, thank you for the spiritual nourishment. It fuels me to pursue my God-given dreams. Vic and Ditas Espanol, Media Ministry family and AJA, thank you for your unending support.

Bo Sanchez, Rissa Singson-Kawpeng, Judith Conception and Marjorie Duterte, thank you for inspiring me to write with love in my heart.

Sherwin Masbate, Manilyn Fernandez, Vanessa Balane, Honey Mae Cuevas, and Vanessa Jane Catulin, thank you for sharing your incredible stories.

Thank you for all the support Collin Garrido, Dana Roiza, Clea Sol Octaviano, Rej Sotabinto, Hazel Gamil, Ma.Flores Valleser, Mhariz Bhoyles, Annabel Dalusung, Hirotaka Noguchi, and Analyn Dano.

To all my friends, thank you for believing in me; for telling me how my articles refresh your spirit. Above all, thank you for your prayers.

Thank you dear readers for walking with me in this journey. May your life be transformed like never before as you turn the pages.

Contents

Introduction	6
Prologue: God's Gift of a Fallen Flower	8
Foreword	10
Chapter 1: A Love so Pure	13
Chapter 2: You are Loved	17
Chapter 3: You are Enough	21
Chapter 4: Sincere and Selfless Love	24
Chapter 5: Die to Yourself	28
Chapter 6: Where do Broken Hearts go?	38
Chapter 7: What it Means to be Pure	43
Chapter 8: It's Never too Late	48
Chapter 9: Pearls of Wisdom for Single Moms	56
Chapter 10: He Loves me, He Loves me not?	67
Chapter 11: Walk on Water	71
Chapter 12: Joy in the Midst of Pain	78
Chapter 13: Glimpse of Heaven	83
Chapter 14: God Chases You	92
Chapter 15: Finding Love God's Way	98
Chapter 16: Conclusion	103

Introduction

- "Am I not pretty enough?"
- "How can I make him love me?"
- "Do I even deserve love?"
- "Is love worth the wait?"
- "Am I worth being pursued?"
- "How do I know if a man really loves me?"
- "How can I move on?"
- "Where do broken hearts go?"
- "Should I lower my standards?"
- "How long should I wait for my one true love?"

These are the questions thrown at me by my friends. I'm not an expert when it comes to relationships so I find it so amusing when a woman sees me as a love guru. I can only thank God for filling me with the power of the Holy Spirit, making me speak such words of wisdom.

"Worth The Chase" was born from an intense calling from God to minister to His beautiful daughters from all corners of the earth. I shed truck-loads of tears before I finally obeyed God's divine leading. At first, I was so scared to give up my corporate job to focus solely on writing. I felt inadequate. Walking out from my comfort zone to the edge of the unknown was one of the toughest decisions I've ever made in my life. But just the thought that women can discover their real worth after reading this book makes it the wisest decision I've made so far.

This book isn't written by me but by God. He used my hands to speak His words of love to all women.

It doesn't matter if you're single, in a relationship (complicated or not), engaged, broken-hearted, a single mom, widow, or married, as long as you hunger for love or if you want to inspire others to look beyond their imperfections, then this book is for you. It includes true stories of real women who used to live in darkness but later found the light of Christ's love.

Introduction

This book isn't just for women! So there ladies, you can buy two or more copies: one for you and one as a gift to your boyfriend. Or save a copy for your future one true love if you haven't got one yet. Don't forget those in your family, friends and workmates whom you feel will be so inspired by this book.

Brendan Roberts, a Catholic missionary and author from New Zealand co-authored this book and equipped with a brilliant mind and the guidance of the Holy Spirit, he wrote the part for men.

Brendan is more than just a mentor to me. He is my bestie, running mate, and prayer buddy. Above all, I see Jesus in him. I shared to Brendan the love letter from God which I wrote at the adoration chapel and since then he has been encouraging me to write at least 5 pages every day to complete this book. It was such a painful task considering that my only time to write was every evening because in the morning I was writing a story for a movie project and I also work as an English teacher to Japanese professionals in the afternoon.

I started writing on February 2, 2015 yet through God's grace, you're reading this book, my first, now! I completed this in 6 weeks! Amazing right? I thought it would take me months or even years to complete this. However, as my life verse goes: "For nothing is impossible with God." (Luke 1:37). I can only look up to the sky and whisper: "I know it's you God!"

Women: May this book bring out the priceless jewel in you. I pray that you realize your real worth not by seeing yourself in the eyes of men but in the eyes of God.

Men: May this book transform you into a man after God's own heart. I pray you lead women closer to God while protecting their purity as well as your own.

All Glory, praise and honor to God Almighty who is Love!

Prologue:
GOD'S GIFT OF A FALLEN FLOWER

The photo of the man I loved with his new girlfriend lingered in my head after seeing it on Facebook. He looked so happy with her. His eyes spoke tremendous love. It hurt me so badly that someone else colored his world. I used to be the woman who made him smile that way.

As tears started welling up in my eyes, I saw two lonely withered flowers sitting next to each other on the ground. Moved with pity, for I saw myself like a flower that has lost its glorious bloom after a terrible heart-break, I picked up the two flowers and felt their delicate petals in my hand.

I looked at the flowers closely and noticed that the other one was infected with ants. I wanted to drop it on the ground but it was too beautiful to let go. The ants started to make their way through the petals and I was fully aware I would get insect bites if I kept holding onto it.

"See? You have to let go of one!" I looked at Brendan, my best friend, who suddenly made such a divinely inspired statement. He was patiently listening to my heart-breaking story while wiping my tears with his shirt.

"You have to let go of one!" Wow! So profound!

I fell silent. Then a man carrying a dustpan passed by, I looked at the flower infected with ants one last time before dumping it, and then I focused my gaze on the other flower left in my hand.

I closed my eyes; tears still streaming down my cheeks. Then suddenly, the wind blew hard, it was strong, yet calm. I knew in my heart it was God, embracing me with His peace, with His love.

Then I understood why God showed me the two fallen flowers, of which I was meant to keep just one. Not all good things are meant to last, because good is often the enemy of the best. The flower infected by ants symbolized the man I loved, the man I had to let go. Just like that flower, no matter how beautiful it was, I have to let go, or else I'll get hurt even more. The ants were the painful memories, biting me until I lost the last thread of hope.

The flower remaining in my hand is the one true love God has been waiting to reveal to me if only I let go of the other one.

Eyes closed, hands clasped to the precious flower in my hand, a soft voice spoke in the depths of my heart…"My daughter, you can't hold onto too many things in your hand. Let go of the past and allow me to surprise you. I have all the blessings in my hand ready for you; please allow me to bring them to you. Surrender your whole life to me. Let me take care of your heart. I will never break it. I will handle it with total care. Your heart may be calloused and full of scars now, yet when you surrender it to me completely, I will make it new, and never forget, my daughter, I've been pursuing you for you are WORTH THE CHASE…"

Foreword

By Brendan Roberts

I am so honored to write the foreword for Elly's first book. It all goes back to that fateful day in December when I saw her in the adoration chapel writing faithfully in a prayer journal. I waited and waited for her to finish. I even went up to the Lord in the Blessed Sacrament, but she didn't notice me as she was so focused. So then I sat at the back of the chapel and wrote on one of my calling cards. I wrote that I'm a Catholic missionary and author and that like me I see that she writes a prayer journal. I left my contact numbers and email address if she wanted to be my friend. Being a beautiful woman, this was a great entry point for me, lol.

I was very surprised when I received a text from Elly, "Hi Bro Brendan. I feel so blessed having to cross your path at St Francis adoration chapel. I love writing that's why I always have my journal with me. I'm thankful to God beyond words. Thank you for approaching me. God bless."

Elly invited me to lunch where we spent two hours chatting as if we were long lost friends. I was very impressed that she gave up her job at God's prompting and took the leap of faith to totally trust Him.

Since meeting Elly I can observe that she has a strong faith and very strong calling to write for women, especially regarding purity and following Christ. It's really remarkable that God brought us together as I too have a calling to write on the subject of purity, which I did as a major theme in my last book, "Crusades Rediscovered: In the Light of Human Sexuality and Our Creator". Elly also has a servant heart and it was truly amazing to see her showing compassion for a friend who is disabled, whom she writes about in this book. She also is a very humble lady, wanting to start a foundation for street children, to give them a better way of life. She has a great sense of humor and as we have become best friends we have had many times laughing together. This has been healing for me as it's not easy being in a country where you don't know the language and your host's workers speak in another language all day.

Elly also has a stubborn streak, meaning she has fights with God and also with other people sometimes. This can be a positive trait as it means she will not turn away from God and the mission of writing that He has placed in her heart.

I have just finished writing a book called "Our Father, Where Art My Pay: A Call to Holiness in the Workplace." When I heard Elly's great testimony of how she was able to share her faith in the workplace I knew I needed to ask her if she would write a chapter about "Faith in the Workplace" for my book. I also knew it was a way to inspire her to start her book.

I was really surprised and humbled when Elly asked me to be her mentor for a project that she discusses later in this book. In fact we became mentors to each other. I encouraged her to write at least 5 pages a day for her book. This meant that she was able to complete it within just 6 weeks. Isn't God amazing?

When Elly would talk to me about her book for women there was a nagging feeling that it shouldn't be just for women. We also became running mates as we would go to a nearby park and run at 6am! After running we would read the Mass readings of the day and share about how they relate to our lives! Then one day after sharing Elly shared with me her vision to have her write, "Worth the Chase" for women and for me to write "Worth Chasing" for men. Wow! I was so excited and so humbled!

So at times I was able to write 5 pages a day and in just six weeks have been able to complete the book. God has given me the grace to focus and the strength to write two books at once and most of all the inspiration to write for this book.

When Elly showed me the love letter from God I was so amazed and touched by it. I knew they were such powerful words and that God would indeed move hearts and change hearts by His grace.

Just to leave you with a mind-blowing thought: It's a double miracle that I met Elly. "Why?" you may ask. Because my first plan was to come to the Philippines for one month only. But through

God's prompting, my host and friend, encouraged me to extend to continue my mission of evangelization. What convinced me was when she generously offered to fund the costs incurred to extend. I extended until 8 December. Then I decided to extend a second time after several people encouraged me and I wanted to be present for Pope Francis' visit. So you could say we weren't supposed to meet but by God's grace we did on 17 December. If not most likely you wouldn't be reading this book now.

Chapter 1

A LOVE SO PURE

"Love is patient, love is kind. It does not envy, it does not boast, it is not proud. It is not rude, it is not self-seeking, it is not easily angered, it keeps no record of wrongs. Love does not delight in evil but rejoices with the truth. It always protects, always trusts, always hopes, always perseveres (1 Corinthians 13:4-7).

It was a spectacular evening in February 14, 2013. Everything around me was perfect: towering mountains; the moon at its brightest; twinkling stars that looked like diamonds in the sky; the graceful movements of the clouds; the birds were chirping and so the air was filled with beautiful music; and oh my knight in shining armor flashed a dashing smile that made my heart flutter. Then he bowed on bended knee before me and asked for my hand. I took his hands into mine feeling volts of electricity shoot through my entire body as his hands touched my waist. Smitten by his loving gaze, we danced to the music of the fast beating of our hearts...

Oh yes, I have a great imagination, right? Before you start thinking that what you're reading now is a fairy tale book written by a hopeless romantic princess, let me tell you what really happened:

Alone and hopeless, (yes there was no knight in shining armor, no birds chirping, nor trace of any other living creatures) I was seated at our rooftop; the wind caressed my face, my heart was as cold as winter's evening breeze as images of my girlfriends with bouquets of flowers and chocolates in both hands flooded my head. I stopped logging into Facebook, choosing to focus my gaze on the walls than get drenched by the cheesy exchange of love notes from those sappy couples on my newsfeed. I uttered bitterly: "Would someone ever love me?" followed by another humiliating voice: "Do I even deserve love?"

I heard a tiny, gentle voice deep within me that said: "Look up" and so I did. I was speechless! Low and behold, right before my very eyes, I saw heart-shaped clouds! My gaze was glued to that beautiful sight on a clear night sky, with my mouth open in awe and wonder of God's majesty! In my heart, I heard God telling me: "Don't you know that I've been longing for you as much as you've been longing for him?"

That very moment I knew that God had been pursuing me all those times that I had been wishing for my so called "Knight in Shining Armor." It's crazy and sad how I wasted too much time wallowing in self-pity each time I saw couples holding hands and wondering when I would be able to hold hands with someone who will perfectly fit mine. I can't count how many times I wished my Prince Charming will come out from the pages of my favorite novel. Little did I know that the true love I had been searching for so long has been available to me even before the world began.

How about you? How long have you been searching for true love? The fact that you are reading this book now, I know deep within you is a child longing for love. I don't know exactly what you've done in the past which makes you think you don't deserve real, authentic love. You might have searched for love in the wrong places. Perhaps you've invested too much time, effort and tears in too many failed relationships. I want you to leave your past behind. Yes, learn from your past failures but don't dwell on them. The mistakes you've made doesn't make God's love for you any less. He sees the future saint in the present sinner. He loves you no matter what and He wants you to experience the perfect love only He can give.

I love looking at the Cross. It makes me realize my worth; my true identity. There's no greater love than Jesus, hanging on the Cross, dying for my sins. He endured pain, suffering and death for my sake, and yes, for your sake, for His love for you. How amazing is that? You are worthy of every drop of Jesus' blood! Jesus lived to die for you. He wore the crown of thorns so you could wear the crown of life!

Now, ask yourself: "Do I even deserve love?" Hear the inner

voice deep within you as you read God's complete knowledge and care from Psalm 139:1-18:

> O LORD, you have searched me and you know me. You know when I sit and when I rise;
> you perceive my thoughts from afar.
> You discern my going out and my lying down;
> you are familiar with all my ways.
> Before a word is on my tongue you know it completely, O LORD.
> You hem me in--behind and before;
> you have laid your hand upon me.
> Such knowledge is too wonderful for me, too lofty for me to attain.
>
> Where can I go from your Spirit?
> Where can I flee from your presence?
> If I go up to the heavens, you are there; if I make my bed in the depths,
> you are there.
> If I rise on the wings of the dawn,
> if I settle on the far side of the sea,
> even there your hand will guide me,
> your right hand will hold me fast.
> If I say, "Surely the darkness will hide me and the light become night around me,"
> even the darkness will not be dark to you;
> the night will shine like the day,
> for darkness is as light to you.
>
> For you created my inmost being;
> you knit me together in my mother's womb.
> I praise you because I am fearfully and wonderfully made;
> your works are wonderful, I know that full well.
> My frame was not hidden from you when I was made in the secret place.
> When I was woven together in the depths of the earth,
> your eyes saw my unformed body.
> All the days ordained for me were written in your book before one of them came to be.
> How precious to me are your thoughts, O God! How vast is the sum of them!
> Were I to count them, they would outnumber the grains of sand. When I awake, I am still with you.

Prayer:

"Father God, thank you for loving me just the way I am; with all my flaws and imperfections. Help me seek you earnestly in prayer so that I may grow in the knowledge of your great love and truth. Let your unfailing love guide me all the days of my life. I love you too Father God. You are my everything."

God's Ways of Love
© Erlita Suarez Cabal

At times when everything seems wrong,
God will hold your hand and tell you to go on;
When you feel like bursting into tears,
He will make you feel that He's always there!

When you are down to nothing,
God is up to something;
Let God heal and let go of your pain,
Let go of your fears and let God sustain!

Say little prayers for little things,
It will fly heavenward on little wings;
No prayer is too great or small,
To ask God who hears them all!

God can reach each falling tears,
He sees the heart that needs a cheer;
He knows the path that's hard and dear,
Don't ever give up because He is near!

Where your strength ends,
The grace of God begins;
You won't face life alone,
His strength will prevail and not your own.

Chapter 2

YOU ARE LOVED

"Greater love has no one than this, that he lay down his life for his friends (John 15:13)."

God knows you from head to toe. His love for you surpasses human understanding. Come to the ultimate source of love. Soak yourself in His presence.

God is gazing at you with love, pure, unabashed, unconditional, eternal, perfect love. He will never lift His gaze off you; He just keeps gazing at you, 24 hours a day.

When you feel like the world is on your shoulders, when you see no glimmer of hope, when you can't find the courage to stand, kneel and tell God: "Father, I'm tired, can you give me a hug?" Close your eyes and feel tremendous peace from His loving embrace.

Just like you, I have my own share of flaws and imperfections. God knows how much I really doubted writing this book. I felt so inadequate. The thought that I don't have the wisdom, skills, and capabilities needed to create a masterpiece that can pierce hearts clouded my mind.

I was losing my balance and I felt the need to surrender my fears. My feet led me to St Francis of Assisi Adoration Chapel, and there, in front of the Holy Eucharist, I acknowledged my weaknesses before a mighty God. I heard God's comforting words, soothing my troubled heart. The next thing I knew, I was already writing a love letter from God, not only to me but to all women.

God kept on dictating His words of love so I was just there, kneeling, writing, crying, not because of sorrow, but because of the tremendous joy I felt in my heart.

You are about to read a letter that can change your life…if you allow it to. Before reading further, open your heart to God's miracles and blessings.

FROM THE VERY HEART OF GOD, TO YOU:

My Daughter,

I love you and I'm proud of you. Yes, you're not perfect but that won't make My love for you any less. You will be made perfect in My love. I love you for who you are. You are My child, My beautiful daughter. Never forget the truth that you belong to Me. Nothing can separate you from My love.

Don't be afraid to fall in love. If he won't catch you if you fall, I will catch you! You are made to love. Don't be afraid to be human. Don't be afraid to be vulnerable. I am here for you. You deserve to be loved! Allow yourself to be loved. Allow yourself to experience the joy that true love brings.

Yes, there will always be an emptiness in your heart. That space is mine. Only I can fill that emptiness.

Every time you doubt about the beauty of My plans for you, just seek My face and My word. I got you My daughter, I will never let you down. Trust in Me. I trust in you. I have created you for a unique and beautiful purpose. Don't stop looking up to Me. I will always be with you.

If only you see yourself the way I see you, then you'll realize you're capable of accomplishing things which are far beyond your imagination.

You are precious in My sight. Take pride in the way I created you. Do not envy others. You are hand-crafted in My image. Rejoice in the way I created you. There's no one else like you in the world. There's a difference only you can make. There's power within you. You are fearfully and wonderfully made. I rejoice in you with singing.

You only have one life to live. Live it well. Keep on pushing. Keep on reaching the dreams I placed in your heart. Nothing is impossible with Me. You see daughter, I have all the blessings in my hands ready for you, and you just need to ask me of it.

I am preparing your heart. Every experience will

make you grow. Stop doubting yourself. If you doubt your capabilities, then you also doubt in My power.

I have given you gifts My child. Every good gift will bring you to your mission. Continue to make a difference in the lives of others. Live for others My child.

Life is beautiful My daughter. I made life so beautiful because I love you. Enjoy every moment as if it's your last. Don't waste your time on worries. Always remember that I'll always take care of you. Cherish everything you have. Never get tired of doing good. Love your family and friends. Reach out to more people. Bring My light to them. I care for the lost as much as I care for you.

Don't focus on yourself alone. Yes, love yourself so you can love others but be selfless. Attend to the needs of others then I'll take care of your own. Take care of your body. Be healthy. Give importance to your physical health as much as you give importance to your emotional and spiritual health.

Be a good steward of My resources. Desire for financial wealth not out from your own selfish motives but with a humble heart that seeks for the betterment of the world and for the welfare of others.

Be a woman I always wanted you to be, a woman after My own heart. Be patient as I mold you. When life gets tough, run to Me. Just one step then I'll be running towards you. I'll chase after you My daughter if you lose your way. That's how much I love you.

You're always in My thoughts and in My heart. There was never a time that I forget about you. You are My priority. Your tears are as important as your laughter. I'm watching your every move. There's a place where you're safe and secure: in my presence.

I love you and NOTHING can change that.

Your Dad,
Almighty God.

Prayer:

"Father God, I come before you, wounded, broken, and crushed. Yet Father, I believe you alone can restore me. Create in me a new heart, a heart that sings praises to you. Help me increase my faith and believe that I am your beautiful daughter, made in your image, hand-crafted delicately by your loving hands, loved, cherished and adored. Help me to see myself the way you see me. Grant me inner healing and peace in Jesus mighty name, Amen."

When The Going Gets Tough
© Erlita Suarez Cabal

My child, I know you're going through a lot,
Always remember that I'm never far apart;
Let me wipe away the tears from your eyes,
I'll add vibrant colors in your gloomy skies!

I saw how tough everything has been,
I am just here, always ready to listen;
I have loved you right from the start,
Your name is whispered in every beating of my heart!

When the road gets tough, hold my hand,
My thoughts towards you are as countless as the sand;
I don't mind that your heart's full of scars,
For to me you are still the brightest star!

When you are frustrated that you want to scream,
Remember that I always believe in your dreams!
Take away all your doubts, in faith, take action!
I created you to be a powerful champion!

Chapter 3

YOU ARE ENOUGH

"For we are God's workmanship, created in Christ Jesus to do good works, which God prepared in advance for us to do (Ephesians 2:10)."

"If only I am prettier, lovelier, taller, sexier..."

"What if my hair is as attractive as the models' hair in a shampoo commercial, would he stop by to feel its soft strands?"

"If only my skin is as soft and supple like the celebrities."

"What if I drive a fancy car and wear glittering jewels, would his eyes be glued to me alone?" [Note from Brendan: No, they will be glued to your jewels, lol.]

"If only I'm as hot as the beauty queens."

I'll be honest with you that those "what ifs" and "if onlys" clouded my head for a time. Influenced by the standard of beauty set by the media and the world, I felt inadequate.

There was a popular superstitious belief in our province that jumping on New Year's Eve once the clock strikes midnight is a great way to grow taller. So every New Year, I would jump as high as I could, silently praying that I would gain at least three more inches. Guess what?! My internal organs suffered dislocation from too much jumping but my height remained at 5'2". I was so envious with my younger sister for she was a lot taller than me. When I told her I wanted to have her height, she told me she would trade her height for my fair skin. It's sad and alarming how women store up so many insecurities in the closet rather than embracing with gratitude the real beauty of God's most captivating creation.

In one of my conversations with God, I asked Him: "Why didn't you make me taller?" His answer was: "I could have made you taller if you were meant to be taller." Wow! His answer blew me away! Kneeling in front of the Holy Eucharist, I felt accepted and loved exactly for who I am. Right there and then, I realized that true womanhood is how I see myself in the eyes of God rather than the eyes of men.

You might have different insecurities than what I have. Maybe you're already tall, curvaceous and pretty, a complete stunner perhaps. But I know at some point in your life, you felt that someone is better than you, whether it be her physical attributes or achievements in life. Maybe you are pressured by other people's high expectations of yourself or worse you're living your life far from who you are really meant to be.

Putting off the beauty of your own uniqueness to please other people spells disaster. Never compare yourself to anyone else. Since you are like no other being ever created since the beginning of time, you are incomparable. You should only compare yourself to the previous you, and from who you were in the past. Get inspired to be a better version of yourself each day.

You are the only you whom God made. Even an identical twin sister won't have the same characteristics as you do. Tell the world you are one-of-a-kind creation who came here to experience wonder and spread joy. The truth is there's a difference only you can make because there's no one like you anywhere in the world.

Don't let anyone tell you that you have to be a certain way, especially if it conflicts with God's ways. Be unique. Be what you feel. You won't be happy if you will always wear a mask. Be your own, unique true self.

Create your own style. Let it be unique for yourself and yet identifiable for others. Don't be afraid to be who you are. Only two things matter: your opinion of yourself and God's opinion of you.

Your uniqueness alone is enough to justify your special place in the world. You must know that you are a miracle, that since the beginning of the world there hasn't been, and until the end of the world there will not be, another like you. You are gifted in a unique and important way. It is your privilege and your adventure to discover your own special light.

You cannot be replaced, nor can your life be repeated. What you bring to the world is completely original and cannot be compared.

Never forget that you are one of a kind. Never forget that if there weren't any need for you in all your uniqueness to be on this earth, you wouldn't be here in the first place.

Prayer:

"Father God, thank you for creating me in your image and likeness. I am forever grateful for the gifts you blessed me with; for the talents you gave me to bless the world.

Help me to see my worth according to your standards and not the standards of this world. Create in me a confident heart; a heart that believes in the truth that we are all your greatest masterpieces."

Delicately Hand-Crafted
© Erlita Suarez Cabal

I have loved you even before you were born,
I took care of you in your mother's womb;
It was my hands which first held you tight,
Oh how precious you are in my sight!

I was there when you let out your first cry,
I witnessed in delight as you flashed your first smile;
When you began to crawl I was guiding you,
I directed your little steps wherever you went.

I cheered you up during your first day at school,
I'm always proud of you, that's for sure!
You are my most treasured possession,
Loving you has always been my passion.

Believe in yourself and do not doubt,
Let the leaves of hope sprout in your heart;
When I remain in you and you in me,
You will be the person I always created you to be.

Chapter 4

SINCERE AND SELFLESS LOVE

"Do not neglect to do good and to share what you have, for such sacrifices are pleasing to God (Hebrews 13:16)."

When was the last time you sacrificed something to make someone happy? I remember a popular commercial on T.V. The guy was about to eat the last piece of biscuit when a hungry, old woman appeared. Though no words were uttered, the expression on her face was a clear sign that she wanted to ask the guy to give up the last piece to at least lessen her hunger.

The guy was moved but as he wanted to savor the last bite he ate half and gave the other half to the woman. As soon as she took it, she transformed into a beautiful genie saying, "Because of your kindness, I can grant one wish". The guy was so surprised and exclaimed excitedly: "I want a red sports car!" A red sports car fell from the sky! But guess what? The sports car only had 2 wheels and half a body, just like the biscuit he gave to the genie in disguise.

I'm sure the guy would have given her the entire biscuit had he known that she was capable of giving him his dream car.

How about you? Do you give from the knowledge that you will gain something in return? What does dying to yourself mean to you?

It was my father who taught me the virtue of being selfless.

"When was the last time you watched a movie in a cinema?" I asked as I looked into my father's expressive eyes. We were watching "Bakit Hindi Ka Crush ng Crush Mo" movie on the big screen. We went out on a date, just the two of us, which my father considered as the best Father's Day treat he had ever received.

"I can't remember the exact date, but I am certain that it was in 1982." He answered, smiling.

"Whoa! That was 33 years ago!" I exclaimed. "Papa, who was with you then? You are my first ever movie date, who's yours?" I teased him.

"Your mom was my girlfriend at that time". His facial expression was that of a man deeply in love.

"Why have you not watched any movies again after that?" My question made my dad silent for awhile.

Then he looked at me and said, "For all those years gone by, my priority has always been working hard to put food on our table and to send you and your siblings to school." It was my turn to be quiet. In my silence, I remembered everything — all the sacrifices my father went through, especially the ones which made me who I am today.

Born into a poor family, I lived my childhood years in a world of fantasy. Yes, fantasy! I had always imagined myself dressed as a princess, living in a white castle (less the Prince Charming thing! Haha).

I used to envy those kids who were born from wealthy parents. There were times I uttered in desperation: "If only my father was a business tycoon, he could buy me all the beautiful dresses and toys of all kinds in the world!" That was my wish to the so-called Fairy Godmother until something happened, something that made me appreciate and love my father all the more.

One day, Papa bought me a new pair of shoes. I remember that I was in grade school. I was excitedly putting them on when I noticed that Papa was wearing a pair of damaged slippers. To imagine how damaged and terrible-looking they were, they were the kind that deserves to be thrown in a garbage bag. (Yeah, you got the right picture in your head!) I asked him: "Why don't you buy a new pair of slippers? I pity your slippers! They're so worn out!"

He answered: "I'm happy to prioritize your needs first before my own. Just by knowing that your delicate feet fit perfectly in your new shoes makes me feel like I'm wearing the most expensive shoes in the world." My heart melted.

Papa has always been with me in my struggles and little triumphs. I can still remember how he shouted "That's my daughter!" as I went up the stage to claim my academic medals. He's the proudest dad and has never missed out any important events in my life. Even if he worked far from home, he has always been there when I received awards from school or when I joined competitions.

One of the fondest childhood memories I had with my father was when I dressed up as an angel for an event in our Church. I was so reckless (well, even until now! Haha) so I ended up breaking one of my improvised angel's wings. I cried and told him I would not be able to fly again. To comfort me, he lifted me up in the air and said that he would be my wings. I sat on his shoulders, closed my eyes, felt the air and pretended that I was flying.

He meant what he said. Since then, he has always been my wings. Each time I feel like quitting, he will always tell me that I can reach my dreams; he believes in me, so I learned to believe in myself.

People questioned him when he decided to send me to college. They were telling me that college education is only for rich people. Though I was a government scholar and I worked during summer vacations to pay for my tuition fee, there were times we fell short of money. During those times, Papa would borrow from neighbors just so I could pay for my exams. Some people would tell him:"You will regret afterwards, your daughter will just get pregnant, she will not be able to graduate." Papa never listened to other people's gossips. He trusted me so much so I did my best; I never wanted to make all his efforts and sweat to be in vain.

When I was hired for my first job, I offered to buy him a new leather wallet as I noticed his wallet had been worn out. He had that wallet for ages. He refused and insisted he would never trade that wallet with anything else. I became so curious as to why the wallet was so precious. So when he wasn't around, I snuck stealthily into his room and checked his wallet, hoping to see what was so valuable inside that he wouldn't allow me to buy him a new one. As soon as I opened it, tears started to flow like a river that never runs dry. Pictures of me (taken when I was still cute and cuddly), my mom and my siblings were glued on it. I finally understood why. Since he had been working away from us, the photos stuck in his wallet would somehow make him feel that we are always with him! I could picture him in his room, taking out his wallet, and looking at his wonderful family each time he missed us.

I deeply regretted those times that I wished I had a different father. If God would give me another lifetime, a chance to choose a father from birth, I would definitely choose him over and over and over again.

My father didn't even have to talk to show me how to die to myself and live for others. His actions taught me how to be selfless. My Dad is God's instrument in building my character. He's the kind of man that will give up anything he has to make others happy.

I bet you've heard the statement, "Actions speak louder than words." Love is a great example. That's exactly what my father did. He didn't have to echo a dreary sermon; he simply showed his love through his actions.

My Papa is the portrait of the Heavenly Father. He loves me so much, with all my warts, wounds, and scars. He accepts me even if I might be the most stubborn daughter. Through his love, I know how I should be treated, respected, and loved by a man. And yes, I can't wait to walk down the aisle while clinging to his strong arms, the same strong arms that held me the first time I took a glimpse of the world outside my mother's womb.

Prayer:

"Father God, thank you for putting me in situations wherein I can give selfless love to others. Thank you for calling me to be your servant. Help me be your hands and feet for those in dire need. This I pray in Jesus mighty name, Amen."

Tell The World Of His Love
© Erlita Suarez Cabal

You are brought to this world for a mission,
Live your life for others and not just for your own;
There's a difference only you can make,
Create a ripple of kindness that will never break.

You are the hands and feet of Jesus,
Everything you do must be in line with His divine purpose;
You are the salt of the earth and the light of this world,
You are to bring to every nation the power of His words.

Chapter 5

DIE TO YOURSELF

"This is how we know what love is: Jesus Christ laid down his life for us. And we ought to lay down our lives for our brothers. If anyone has material possessions and sees his brother in need but has no pity on him, how can the love of God be in him? Let us not love with words or tongue but with actions and in truth (1 John 3:16-18)."

When do you feel the most loved? When someone says "I love you" over and over? Or when someone shows you love by treating you kindly or helping you? The words "I love you" are certainly sweet to hear, but without action they are meaningless.

I know you want to love and be loved—that's just how God made you. By showing love to others, you exemplify God's love for you. God's very character is love, and one of the reasons He sent His Son was to show you how to love.

Serving others unselfishly; sharing your life and your resources; helping others; sacrificing for those around you; and encouraging each other are all ways you can show the love Jesus taught and lived. Then your actions will truly speak louder than your words.

That is exactly what Jesus meant when He said:

> "What good is it, my brothers, if someone says he has faith but does not have works? Can that faith save him? If a brother or sister is poorly clothed and lacking in daily food, and one of you says to them, 'Go in peace, be warmed and filled,' without giving them the things needed for the body, what good is that? So also faith by itself, if it does not have works, is dead." (John 2:14-17).

The same Bible verse pierced my heart when I saw an old man on the street. He was dressed in shabby clothes. I was determined to just pass him by but I heard God's voice: "Give him your jacket, he needs it." I immediately answered God: "No way! Not my favorite, new leather jacket!"

I wanted to run and just ignore the old man but my conscience won the battle. After fighting with God I approached the man and still with hesitation, I handed over my favorite possession.

He smiled and exclaimed: "Oh! Thank you! I'll give this to my wife, she badly needs this." So that was why God urged me to give it to him; God used my jacket as an instrument for him to show his love for his wife. I could have missed the blessing of being an instrument in answering someone else's prayer had I not obeyed God!

How about you? How many times have you heard God's voice asking you to lend a hand to the needy? Did you ignore His voice?

You might say: "What I have is just enough for me, how can I give to others?" Even the poorest of the poor has something to give. There's no such thing as "nothing to give". I want you to ponder on the story of the poor widow:

> "Jesus sat near the Temple treasury, he watched the people as they dropped in their money. Many rich men dropped in a lot of money; then a poor widow came along and dropped in two little copper coins, worth about a penny. He called His disciples together and said to them, "I tell you that this poor widow put more in the offering box than all the others. For the others put in what they had to spare of their riches; but she, poor as she is, put in all she had – she gave all she had to live on." (Mark 12: 41-44)

Reflect: If the poor widow had two little copper coins, what do you have?

Let me tell you another story of a poor widow:

> Then the Lord said to Elijah, "Go and live in the village of Zarephath, near the city of Sidon. I have instructed a widow there to feed you." So he went to Zarephath. As he arrived at the gates of the village, he saw a widow gathering sticks, and he asked her, "Would you please bring me a little water in a cup?" As she was going to get it, he called to her, "Bring me a bite of bread, too." But she said, "I swear by the Lord your God that I don't have a single piece of bread in the house. And I have only a handful of flour left in the jar and a little

cooking oil in the bottom of the jug. I was just gathering a few sticks to cook this last meal, and then my son and I will die." But Elijah said to her, "Don't be afraid! Go ahead and do just what you've said, but make a little bread for me first. Then use what's left to prepare a meal for yourself and your son. For this is what the Lord, the God of Israel, says: There will always be flour and olive oil left in your containers until the time when the Lord sends rain and the crops grow again!" So she did as Elijah said, and she and Elijah and her son continued to eat for many days. There was always enough flour and olive oil left in the containers, just as the Lord had promised through Elijah (1 Kings 17: 8-16).

Reflect: If the poor widow had a handful of flour and a little cooking oil, what about you?

You see, when God sees the desire in your heart to help, He will supply you with all the resources you need. I can testify to this.

I and my friends were planning to celebrate my 24th birthday at Tahanan ng Pagmamahal, (an orphanage founded by Bo Sanchez, a Catholic lay preacher and best-selling author). A week before my birthday celebration, I had to pay off my sister's tuition fee so I planned to cancel the celebration due to financial problems but God poured out His blessings upon me. The unexpected happened. Clea, a great friend of mine who loves cooking and is a really good cook, offered to cook for the kids. Not just that she even bought toiletries and gift items. Clarice, another great friend, offered to sponsor balloons and other birthday decorations. I received a call from Miles, another close friend whom I met from a life-changing Love Life retreat, telling me that she would drop by at my dorm to donate toys. My cousin Geralvin prepared loot bags for the kids. My then boyfriend sent cash to help me with all the other expenses. I was overwhelmed by the support I received from everyone around me.

The celebration came and everything was perfect. My housemates woke up very early in the morning just to help with cooking and all the other preparations. I told my friends not to give me gifts but to bring goodies for the kids instead. Surprisingly, I still received birthday presents. I got a huge bouquet of pink stargazers from my former officemates and I had three birthday cakes! I had seriously considered canceling the celebration but God had great plans in mind.

When the program was about to end, one of the kids gave me a beautiful birthday message. He thanked all of us for making them happy. Oh yes, how can I forget their innocent smiles? That day was one of my best birthday celebrations ever! It was a day full of laughter, and yeah, tears as well, tears of unexplainable joy!

God is really a God of surprises! Now, will you allow Him to surprise you too?

Prayer:

"Father God, you lived and died for me, help me to live and die for you too. Teach me your ways. Create in me a heart that cares for other people's welfare. Use me to bless the world. Help me seek you earnestly in prayer.

Let me walk where you walked. Let your unfailing love overflow in my heart so I can radiate pure, authentic love. Let my hands be your hands, my feet your feet. Guide my eyes; help me recognize those who need my help. Teach me to obey you. Allow my heart to find joy in giving. Develop in me a heart of gratitude. Let my lips sing praises to you. Help me die to myself and live for others. This I pray in Jesus mighty name, Amen."

Waif
© Erlita Suarez Cabal

Somber eyes about to shed tears,
Hopeless heart full of fears;
Tame face distorted from too much weeping,
Sordid, gaunt hands tired of begging.

No other choice but to be contented with shabby clothes,
Body shaking from fever, cough and colds;
There's no way of finding a safe shelter,
That's the painful reality of being a pauper.

Nothing left in hand but a single penny.
Time seems to pass by so slowly;
What's audible are only those slamming doors,
Leaving a faint growl in silent rancor.

Why are you pretending to be blind?
When you know the right thing is to be kind?
Isn't it better to see hopeful, shimmering eyes,
Rather than hearing shriek of countless deep, sorrowful sighs?

Bonus:

SPIRITUAL WISDOM FOR EVERY HEART

Whatever your status is, read on! I have a very reliable source: the Holy Spirit (with my hopeless romantic heart!)

SINGLE:
Men: Be a man after God's own heart. Have the courage to be the right man your ideal woman would love to spend the rest of her life with. As soon as you pursue her with clarity, develop and discern the relationship process.

Women: Make your heart so hidden in God that a man has to seek Him first just to find you. Don't forget to work on being Miss Right, that is, to be the woman God created you to be.

IN A RELATIONSHIP:
Men: Self-control, patience and sacrifice are the virtues that make relationships last. If your heart is sure that she is the one, like for any woman in your life, guard her purity as well as your own. Your princess should not be just the object of your affection; she's way more than that, so treat her as such. Shower her with sincere compliments.

Women: Glorify God with your body. Know that you are worth being respected as you are God's beautiful princess. Don't be too hard on your man if he falls short from the leading men in movies; don't expect that he is from the pages of your favorite novel. Bring out the best in him instead by leading Him closer to God.

GETTING MARRIED:
Men: Before planning out the best proposal you could possibly make, talk to God first. Choosing a lifetime partner is one of the most important decisions in life. Are you ready physically, spiritually, emotionally, and financially?

Women: Oh yeah! It's one of the best feelings in the world! When your man finally kneels down and asks for your hand in marriage! Don't get too focused on the wedding preparations like how fabulous you will appear on your wedding day. Know that a happy bride radiates beauty that glows from within. The wedding and the reception will last for only a few hours. The marriage will last for the rest of your life. Above all else, prepare your heart.

JUST MARRIED:
Men: In marriage, you'll savor what real life is after the honeymoon stage. Everything will not be as smooth-sailing as the first days. Be prepared for greater challenges! While you are living under the same roof, you might discover qualities that are far from ideal. You have to remember that if you can't accept her at her worst, then you don't deserve her best. Be grateful that she has chosen you for a lifetime.

Women: Marriage is a walk on the path of roses with thorns. If you feel like your love story becomes far distant from the fairy tale you expected it to be, then believe that it is God who writes your love story, and so it will be the best story ever written. Never allow any setbacks to make you fall into a trap of regret. After all, you chose your spouse, so decide to love him forever, no ifs and no buts.

MARRIED FOR YEARS:
Men: Instead of looking for a younger version of your wife, look back to that first moment when you could not even take your gaze off her. Her wrinkled face is nothing compared to the joy she brought to your life. Make every day a Valentine's Day. Take her out on a date, do the things you used to do when you were still courting her. Courtship doesn't end when she finally said yes. Make your love for her grow stronger each day.

Women: Take care of yourself. Make an effort to look desirable for your husband. Being busy at work and having kids aren't justifiable excuses not to look your best. If you don't want your husband eying someone else, then make his eyes glued on you. [Note from Brendan: But don't you dare use super-glue, lol] Above anything else, don't forget to maintain the beauty of your character; it's the kind of beauty that doesn't fade with time. Be faithful to him until you breathe your last.

SEPARATED/DIVORCED:
Men: Evaluate why the relationship ended; don't just simply blame your partner. Chances are, both of you have committed your own share of mistakes. If she has cheated on you as the reason for the breakup, hate the sin but not the sinner. Ask God if there will still be a way out to redeem the relationship. If the answer is no, instead of focusing on finding a new love, focus on striving to still be the best father to your kids. Don't run away from your respon-sibilities.

Women: Your worth is not determined by the failed relationship. Forgive yourself. This is the first step to forgiving your partner for whatever reason that has caused the downfall of your relationship. Be the best mother that you can be. Engage on activities that would boost your self-esteem. Touch other people's lives. Comfort other women who are going through what you have gone through in the past. Don't keep grudges in your heart.

SINGLE BLESSEDNESS:
Men: If God has called you to live a celibate life, then be happy about it. Make the Church your bride. Feel the everlasting joy of bringing many souls to heaven. It is God who put the desire in your heart to be a shepherd of His flock; following His will is the best decision ever! You have Him as your greatest reward.

Women: Seeking God is the greatest adventure. Finding God is the greatest fulfillment. Falling in love with God is the greatest romance. As you grow in your undistracted service with the Lord, you will come to realize that you really don't need a man to complete you. Christ is more than enough. His love surpasses any affection a man could offer.

IT'S COMPLICATED: Below are the "complicated" (it's just really simple, what we do makes it complicated! Haha) situations:

IN LOVE WITH SOMEONE WHO IS ALREADY COMMITTED TO SOMEONE ELSE:
Men: Hey dude! She's not the only woman left in the world! [Note from Brendan: No kidding!] If you really love her, then let her be happy with her man. Love is not about owning a relationship; it's about being guiltless knowing you didn't

take away someone from anybody else. Prepare to be the best man for the right woman God has prepared for you.

Women: Just because he doesn't have his eyes on you doesn't mean you are not lovable or desirable enough. Don't get jealous with the girl he chooses to love just because she colors his world now. Believe that a man will come along, someone who will rock your world as you rock his. Wait for your own love story to blossom.

MUTUAL UNDERSTANDING (M.U):
Men: Lay down your intentions. Don't make her fall in love with you if you're not yet ready for commitment. If the relationship has no label whatsoever, and you don't have any plans taking it to the next level, then don't make her feel so special that she thinks you love her. Treat her as you would treat any other women, as a friend. Make sure you define the relationship.
Women: Don't give him false hopes and don't assume as well. If he has been treating you as if you're his girlfriend, don't be afraid to ask what you mean to him. Never play with each other's emotions. Say no to "friends with benefits". Make sure you have a clear answer to this question: "Is he just testing the waters?"

IN LOVE BUT JUST CAN'T TELL:
Men: Rejection is way better than regret. Common! Tell her how much she means to you. Who knows? Maybe she's just waiting for you to spill it out! Don't hold back. Don't wait until you see her with someone else. You know deep in your heart that she's worth pursuing. Speak up or forever hold your peace.

Women: Most often than not, it is taboo for a woman to be the first one to spill the beans. However, if his actions have been bothering you for quite awhile and you feel that both of you feels the same way, then dare to tell him the truth about how you feel. It's not being flirty; it's just freeing yourself from the many questions in your heart that has been haunting you for so many nights.

LONG DISTANCE RELATIONSHIP:
Men: Be faithful. Don't turn your attention to someone else just because she is far from you. Be grateful that you have someone so special to miss. Keep the communication strong.

Make an effort to let her feel loved even from a distance. You may be one day further from the last time you saw each other, yet closer to her the next time you will.

Women: Trust him. Don't dwell on useless suspicions. When you long for the feeling of being taken care of and you get tempted to entertain some other guys who are just next to you, remember that love knows no distance. It means so little when someone means so much. As long as you share the same sky, you're still together.

STILL IN LOVE WITH AN EX:
Men: If she doesn't love you anymore, move on by surrendering her and your heartache to God! Believe that someone will come along to steal your heart. Don't get even by courting another woman you don't really love. Heal the pain first before jumping into another relationship. If you know she still loves you and there's still a chance to win her back, then do all your best to make it happen.

Women: If you still love him, then be honest about it but don't try to win him back without making sure that he still loves you too or else you're bound for another heart-break. When it's clearer than the blue sky that he's really not that into you, then let go. To let go is to be thankful of the experiences that made you laugh, cry, and grow. It's about all that you have, all that you had and all that you will soon gain. Letting go is to open a door, to clear a path and set yourself free. Moreover letting go is to surrender to the Loving Father so that He can surprise you with even more blessings and challenges in your life.

BROKEN-HEARTED: (FOR WHATEVER REASONS NOT MENTIONED ABOVE)
Men: The pain in your heart cannot be washed away by buckets of beer. Don't hold back your tears. Real men do cry. Surrender your bravado. Acknowledge what you feel. You are likely to get into serious trouble if you prefer to get drunk just to forget how you feel. Yes, you may forget for awhile but as soon as you wake up, the wound is still there. Talk to God and surrender her and your heartache. He is close to the broken-hearted.

Women: Cry all you want but after that, pick up the broken pieces of your life. Smile because it happened. A heart-break is a blessing. After each heart-break you will come out stronger and wiser. Be beautiful inside and out. In the process of healing your wounded heart, make Jesus Christ your boyfriend. Rest assured He will wipe away every single tear from your eyes. Surrender your heartache and him to the Lord. Don't be afraid to fall in love again. It's better to love and get hurt than never to have loved at all.

If you think I missed out on your current status now, then email me at worththechase2@gmail.com so I can chase after Cupid for us to discuss your case. Just kidding! It's best for you to talk to God. He is an expert when it comes to relationships.

Whatever your status is, be happy! *Fix your eyes on Jesus. He is the best lover!* There is no greater love than Him hanging on the cross, dying for your sins. *You are loved, cherished and adored. There is nothing that can separate you from His love.*

"For I am convinced that neither death nor life, neither angels nor demons, neither the present nor the future, nor any powers, neither height nor depth, nor anything else in all creation, will be able to separate us from the love of God that is in Christ Jesus our Lord (Romans 8:38-39)."

Chapter 6

WHERE DO BROKEN HEARTS GO?

"The Lord is close to the broken-hearted and saves those who are crushed in spirit (Psalm 34:18)."

If at some point in your life you experienced mending a wounded heart, or are still in the process of moving on, then this chapter is for you. Or it's also pertinent if you want to know how to keep your sanity when time comes that your heart gets broken.

When was the last time you cried over spilled milk? I mean, over a failed relationship?

"I'm a certified NBSB (No Boyfriend Since Birth) but my heart got broken many times than I could count." Honey Mae shared her sentiments with me. Honey is an awesome friend whom I met at a life-transforming retreat for singles, Love Life retreat.

Confused, I asked her: "Is that because you're the only one who's aware that you two are in a relationship? You know, the 'he's-my-boyfriend-but-he-doesn't-know' kind of thing?"

She laughed and recalled how many times she cried when she saw the "man of her dreams" courting another woman or having a fantastic relationship with someone else while she cried silently.

There was one instance she fell in love with her best friend. She thought he felt the same; he told her to wait for him. She waited four long, painful years only to find out he was engaged to someone else.

She uttered bitterly: "You know what Elly, the hardest part of being in love with my best friend is watching him fall in love with someone else while I have to sit back, watch, and be happy for him."

Ouch! That was painful! I have experienced it myself. Well, I have my own fair share of loving and letting go, of weeping and wiping the tears away.

I had my heart broken the first time 7 years ago. I cried myself to sleep and woke up with my pillow saturated with tears; every part of me was slowly breaking apart; crushed to tiny pieces; my then tender heart became calloused with too much pain. Every inch of my being longed for him; the thought of him with someone else haunted me for so many nights.

Wait! Does that ring a bell? I bet you felt the same way, when the love story you thought would be a "happily ever after" was fading away right before your very eyes. Your world shattered, your mind filled with questions left unsaid and heart screaming with emotions you kept deep within. Don't worry, you're not alone.

I'm willing to share the wisdom I gained from nursing a wounded heart. The scar remains, yet the lessons I learned are worth the throbbing pain. Life goes on for me, and so for you.

Let me share with you an article I wrote when I was 18, the first time I shed tears for a guy:

Stealthy Glances

> "The best part of being in love is when you just love a person and be happy about it, even if that person can never be yours, even if you know it can't last forever! That's the true essence of love. It's not about winning someone; it's not about owning a relationship. It's about being happy because you know you've loved someone. It's about being guiltless because you know you didn't take away someone from anybody. You just love and love unselfishly."

"Oh! Really? Why would I go on loving if I know that the one I love can never be mine? That's unfair! It's not the best part of being in love! I could imagine the terrible pain if you love someone and then you know he can never be yours! That's foolishness!" I first reacted after reading that love quote; I was against it until I was trapped in the following situation…

By sophomore year my life revolved on a daily basis around class, home, then bed. There was no time for anything else. Then I was running to my next class when a cute guy suddenly grabbed my attention.

"Hi" he greeted me as he flashed his most dashing, alluring smile. I lost my voice. All I could think of was how completely messed up I looked in my slightly ironed university uniform. To me, combing my hair was a painful task. I wasn't the kind of girl that would spend an hour or more in front of the mirror just to make sure everything's in proper place, from socks to perfect hair locks.

"Would you like to join my club? You can register now!" He broke the silence, still smiling.

Without saying a word and not even looking at what sort of a club it was, I wrote my name on the registration sheet he gave me and remembering I was late for my class, I left him but the memory of his smile never left me.

That wasn't my first and last encounter with him. I joined his club, which I later discovered was a religious organization for the youth called CFC Youth For Christ. Admittedly, I joined just so I could be with him often. I didn't know then that God had been working with my heart. Getting me to join Youth For Christ was one of the techniques God used in pursuing me.

The first time I saw him playing the guitar while leading us into worship, I was completely smitten. My eyes were glued on him alone. It was as if it was just myself and him inside the room. There was one time he reserved a seat for me in the front row. What he did touched my heart. Oh my gosh! I liked him a lot. He never failed to show me that he cared. As I got to know him each passing day, I realized he had the qualities any girl would admire: handsome, talented, and intelligent, a head-turner indeed; someone who can win any girl's heart just by his mere smile.

I couldn't remember when and how I started liking him; maybe it was from the very first time I saw him. I kept a diary dedicated entirely for him; I wrote about every moment we spent together, be it inside the prayer room or outdoors having youth camps.

For a time, I was hooked in romantic fantasies, felt sparkling moments, imagined and presumed things.

Days passed by. Since in the past I liked guys whom I knew for a short time I thought I was over him, that he was nothing else than a cute guy on my crush list! But something happened which drew us together; we became close friends.

I was disturbed by his presence. I didn't know how to deal with him. I didn't know how to act when he was near so I asked myself: "If I am through with my feelings for him then why do I feel this way? Oh God! I'm already falling for this guy!"

Before I knew it, my world became topsy-turvy. When he walked towards me, it made me stand still. I felt some thrill through my spine when he passed me by just to say "hi". I shivered whenever he was near and when he talked to me I couldn't help but stammer.

He never failed to make my heart skip a beat, making me feel so jittery. I didn't know the feeling existed. I didn't even care that my friends were calling me "dummy". His smile threatened to burst my very heart, and just the sound of his voice filled me with so much happiness. Being with him made me feel cozy, yet dizzy.

I was in the midst of those teenage romantic feelings when I saw him with someone; with a spark of love in their eyes. A scene of them holding their hands, whispering words of love [Note from Brendan: What!! Were you eaves dropping? lol] as if it was just the two of them in this crazy world crushed me into thousands of pieces. [Note from Brendan: Oh Elly that must have really hurt having your heart broken]. I began hating myself for thinking that he liked me too, the way he treated me, the way he looked at me. Why on earth did I mistake it as love? Everything was clear to me, he only saw me as a dear friend. That hurt but I pretended to be okay. I smiled to cover up the pain and laughed to cover up the hurt.

The quote about the best part of being in love came rushing to my head. Then I realized, yes, it's true, that's the best part of being in love. True love is unselfish. When you love, you care not only for your own sake but for the happiness of the one you love. Having that realization, I smiled a genuine smile, not pretentious anymore.

Then I told myself: "Why would I worry so much? What then if he can't be mine? At least I'm not taking him from someone; I just can't let my heart stop loving him. I know, I don't have to be popular or change to someone I'm not because someone may have loved me or will soon love me just the way I am. Not only accepting me for who I am but also for who I am not."

In the end, my first heart-break gave me happiness. It was when I realized that God knew how I felt and He knew what is best for me that I had the courage to let him go. Yes, I failed in making him fall for me but I didn't have to do that in the first place.

Now I know I just have to be someone worthy to love and the rest is up to the man. From then on I felt contented simply by being his friend; secretly hoping that he didn't notice the shadows of love in my stealthy glances.

Likewise, let your past love and experience make you better, not bitter. All broken hearts go back to God, to be repaired by Him and made new if you let Him.

Prayer:

"Father God, thank you for healing my brokenness; for binding up my wounds and for putting all the tiny pieces of my heart together. Help me believe that every heart-break is a gift from you; may I see it as your way of saving me for the right person you prepared for me."

The Art Of Letting Go
© Erlita Suarez Cabal

To let go isn't to think about, ignore, or forget,
It doesn't leave feelings of anger, jealousy, or regret;
Letting go isn't about winning or losing,
Letting go is learning, experiencing, and growing.

It's not about pride and not about how you appear,
It is not obsessing or dwelling on what you used to hold dear;
Letting go isn't about blocking a beautiful memory,
But to open a door, clear a path and set yourself free!

Letting go doesn't leave emptiness, hurts, and sadness,
To let go is to be thankful for the experiences;
It's not about giving in or giving up,
It is about creating a brand new start!

To let go is to cherish the memories but to overcome and move on,
It's about all that you had, and all that you will gain soon;
It is having an open mind with confidence in the future,
It is about clinging to God more.

Chapter 7

WHAT IT MEANS TO BE PURE

"Do you not know that your body is a temple of the Holy Spirit, who is in you, whom you have received from God? You are not your own; you were bought at a price. Therefore honor God with your body (1 Corinthians 6:19-30)."

I have a dark past. I'm no saint yet, though I'm continuously striving to be one. I was in a wrong relationship. Although we didn't go all the way, we did things which were not pleasing to God. I dishonored my body: the temple of the Holy Spirit.

At the start of the relationship, I made it clear to him that one of my greatest dreams is to walk down the aisle pure. He didn't agree with my terms and conditions; he told me I was being too hard on myself and on him. He convinced me that sex will bring the relationship to its highest level, that it would create a wonderful bond of intimacy between lovers.

I was surrounded with so called liberated friends. They openly talked about their sexual experiences and often I was ridiculed for my decision to wait until marriage. I was told it's okay to give in, that I won't lose anything in the process but will savor unexplainable pleasure instead.

I've seen women jumping from one relationship to another; giving themselves entirely to every man they will have an intimate relationship with. In my eyes they seemed happy doing all those things, so I believed in a lie that I would be just fine doing the same.

Pressured by my friends' demands to try explore new things, I finally agreed for a first kiss from my then boyfriend. I was 22 when I had my first kiss, and yes, admittedly, it felt good. So good, that I craved for more than just a kiss. Somewhere deep within me, I felt that I was doing something wrong but I brushed it off and told myself: "It's just a kiss, it won't hurt." But hey ladies, let's get real, everything starts with just a kiss right?

The kiss started with a quick smack on the lips which later developed into a long, passionate kiss. That was the first time I felt strange emotions, a mixture of excitement and thrilling anticipation. These were feelings I had never felt before. My knees became like jelly and I was almost at the precipice, ready to give in but somewhere deep within my soul was screaming, fighting and pulling me out from the darkness that engulfed me. It was the voice of God.

Tears began to well up in my eyes as I pushed my then boyfriend away. He didn't want to stop; he showered me with kisses instead and pulled me back even harder. I was so tempted to remain in his arms but God was stronger than my wrong sexual desires. With tears streaming down my face, I bravely told him: "If you really love me, you will respect my body."

He looked at me in disbelief as if I had uttered magical words, casting a spell on him. A tear drop fell from his eyes. He stopped and kissed my forehead. When he left, I ran to the bathroom. I locked myself in there for three hours, crying until it felt the source of my tears had run dry.

Some of my friends were sexually active, so I figured that as long as I kept my virginity, I was good. Next my boyfriend said he respected my decision to remain pure and that he was willing to wait until the wedding night. But he told me I owed him other sexual favors since I was holding out on him. He said that it was perfectly normal for a man like him to have sexual needs and that if I wanted to keep him, then I should give him something sexual. Little by little, I gave him everything he wanted except my virginity. It felt so wrong, but I consoled myself by comparing with other friends, that they were doing worse things. If only I recognized that I was being used, not loved. That was the bitter outcome of comparing our relationship with those in worse relationships.

It was by God's grace that I was able to save my virginity. However, that has something to do only with physical purity.

There were many times that I allowed my mind to be filled with lustful thoughts. I imagined myself making love with the man of my dreams. It felt wrong, but I consoled myself by assuring that it wouldn't go as far as doing it for real. I told myself that it was just in my mind, that it wouldn't cause any harm.

Pornography became my lover when I broke up with my boyfriend. At first I thought it was perfectly fine as I thought that everyone does it in private. I failed to recognize that it was eating me up; it ruined my emotional and spiritual purity. My heart wasn't pure anymore.

I convinced myself repeatedly that I was better compared to many other women who were engaged in sexual activities outside marriage. "At least I'm not sleeping with a man, I'm not giving in totally, and I'm not hurting anyone". This was how I justified myself each time I read porn articles. But, was I really hurting no one? Why did I hear a tiny voice deep within me say: "You're hurting Me"?

The mere fact that I did those things in private is a clear sign that I wasn't proud of what I was doing. After each lustful article or video, I spent most of my time convincing myself that what I did was perfectly normal. Then I said to myself if it was no big deal at all, then there was no need to convince myself in the first place.

"If you're right, why are you doing it in the dark and not in broad daylight?" the tiny voice in my heart whispered.

Then I discovered one truth that blew me away. The truth comes from Psalm 139:2-3: "You know everything I do; from far away you understand all my thoughts. You see me, whether I am working or resting; you know all my actions."

Wow! God knows everything! He sees even the things I do in secret! That made me feel so ashamed of myself. I stopped... for awhile. The sin was so tempting and alluring that I kept on craving for it and I failed in fighting the battle of temptations, not once but many times. What was I doing wrong? Why did I fail even after knowing that God sees everything I do? That's because I didn't realize that I don't just have to fight temptation, I need to run away from it!

I didn't understand the gravity and the serious nature of the sin so I wasn't that motivated in pursuing a life of holistic purity.

It takes surrendering to God and the Sacrament of Reconciliation for inner healing. The last time I succumbed to the sin of lust, I ran to the Holy Eucharist in adoration. I wept on bended knee and listened to God's soothing voice; His beautiful words comforted my soul.

Kneeling, with tears in my eyes, I wrote what He said to me, His love letter to me about overcoming temptations. I believe this letter is not just for me, but also for you:

My Daughter,

Stop sinning. Stay away from your favorite sin. Would you trade a lifetime of happiness just for a few seconds of fleeting and sinful pleasure? You deserve more than temporary pleasure. You deserve true love. Fight the fire of lust's pleasures with the fire of My word.

How can you preach about purity if you yourself are not pure in your mind, heart, and spirit? Remember that purity is not just about your body but your whole being.

Respect yourself. Run away from temptation. Don't let the enemy lure you. Be patient as I mold you. You will experience the true joy of your sexuality within the Sacrament of Marriage. Believe me, it's worth-waiting for.

Never listen to the enemy's lies again. Be strong and courageous against the call of the flesh. I designed your sexuality for a beautiful purpose and that is for procreation.

Sex is holy and beautiful. Don't allow the world's standards to distort its real essence.

I still love you. Be inspired by My love for you to overcome temptations.

Your Dad,
Almighty God.

As I turned my back on lust, I discovered that true pleasure is something only God can give. I experienced the true joy of loving myself the way God wants me to when I decided to live a life pleasing to Him.

If you have given up your virginity already, don't worry, there is great hope! You can still regain your purity and become a spiritual virgin. Read the next chapter to find out how.

Prayer:

"Father God, help me look only to You and to how I measure up to Your standard and not to this world. Help me treat my body as a gift to be guarded, a gift that can be given only with a wedding ring and the lifelong commitment of true love that comes with it."

Treasure Your Body
© Erlita Suarez Cabal

Your body is a gift from Me,
It's not meant for any relationship or just any old day;
It's meant for the big day when you say "I do"
Don't compromise My best for you.
Your body is valuable for you are my treasure,
Don't soak yourself in fleeting pleasure;
Your body is a gift to be opened by the right person,
Don't trade eternal happiness with just a moment of passion…

Don't give in to the standards of this world,
Fight the fire of lust with the fire of My word;
My spirit dwells within you,
Only in Me you will find a love so pure, so true.

Chapter 8

IT'S NEVER TOO LATE

"If we confess our sins, he is faithful and just and will forgive us our sins and purify us from all unrighteousness (1 John 1:9)."

Are you living in the past that you forget to look forward to the beauty of the future and the gift of today?

Do you not trust that you can still have a brighter tomorrow no matter how dark your past is?

Are the wrongs of yesterday hindering you from doing what is right today?

Do you believe in your heart that God has forgiven you?

Are you still holding onto regrets caused by bad choices and wrong decisions?

Do you doubt that you still deserve to be loved?

Do you think you are worthless because of the past?

Let me share with you an incredible story of my beautiful friend Ada. Read her story and allow God to move you to tears. I saw her deep desire to inspire women through her dark, painful past.

A Second Chance
By Ada

This is a true story of a beautiful woman who loses her true identity and later finds her self-worth in God.

Eyes half-closed, I managed to walk awkwardly on my high heels towards the couch. Though dizzy and exhausted from a crazy night out, I still recognized the disturbing fact that I wasn't inside my room.

My head was spinning and that made it even worse. The spirit of alcohol made both my flesh and spirit weak. I was drunk yet completely aware of the strong arms embracing me. I tried to push him away but my weak arms were nothing compared to his masculine prowess. His fresh scent flavored with the sweet and captivating aroma of wine filled my nostrils.

"Stop..." I whispered softly.

"I love you" he responded.

When he whispered those words, my world stood still. I shook my head and pinched my cheeks to make sure I wasn't dreaming. I thought to myself: "Is this for real? Someone just said he loves me? WOW!" In a split second, my painful childhood years, and my dark past flashed back...

I grew up with a twin sister. Her name is *insecurities*. Going to school was the last thing I wanted to do because as the bullies told me, I was neither beautiful nor smart enough. Because of that I envied every single person in the world.

I had few friends in grade school and for me, I was the ugliest. During Christmas parties, my classmates were wearing new and expensive clothes while I had no other choice but to wear my Mom's loose blouse and old pants.

Something happened when I was in high school. I was awarded a scholarship in a private school and I thought my situation would drastically change but I was wrong. It was so disappointing to know that even if I studied in a private school, the way people saw me remained the same: a poor, ugly girl. Most of my classmates were rich. They could afford to buy the most expensive gadgets, while I could not even afford to buy my own books.

I failed to maintain my grades and so I was transferred to a public school. Surrounded by wrong sets of friends, I was influenced to try lots of things that a student shouldn't be doing. I was hooked to the fleeting pleasures of smoking, drinking, cutting classes, watching porn and cheating during exams.

I was seeking for attention so I enjoyed having a number of boyfriends at the same time. I thought that my self-worth depends on the quantity of boyfriends I had.

My self-worth vanished again when my cousin's boyfriend molested me. I was afraid to tell anyone because I knew that no one would believe me. I didn't even tell my parents about it. My Dad wouldn't care anyway, or so I thought. I never heard him say that he was proud of me. Well, I was used to that and that's the reason why I kept my distance from my own father...

Memories of the past suddenly evaporated when I felt a soft kiss on my cheek. From the painful memory I chose to bury in my heart, I was back to the couch where I was clasped by strong arms, weakening all my senses.

At first I refused my lover's kiss but he whispered the magic words "I love you Ada" over and over again. It was music to my ears. Those were words that I had been longing to hear. I got carried away and at a very young age, I lost my virginity.

When I got home, every single detail of the terrible thing I did haunted me. I felt so dirty. I ran to the bathroom, I scrubbed my body with great force, as if I could remove the trace of my weakness. I wept knowing that I had lost something I would never gain back.

I wished it was the first and the last but it wasn't. I fell in love with him. No one cared for me the way he did. I found the acceptance that I had been longing for so long. He somehow quenched the thirst of the unsatisfied child in me.

He asked me to stop working and so we decided to live together in his condominium. He showered me with everything I needed. I got all the things I wished for when I was a child. There were times I asked myself if I really loved him or I just thought so because of the benefits I was getting. It was like "I give you my body, so give me your money".

Everything seemed perfect yet we both knew from the very beginning that our relationship would never last. He could give me all the material things in the world but he would never give me the most important thing — MARRIAGE.

I knew in my heart that I would never be his bride. Sad but true, the man whom I had given my virginity, and the one whom I was living with in sin was MARRIED WITH TWO KIDS. Yes, I was his mistress.

Each time we had been together, I tried so hard to convince myself that everything was just okay, that we were not doing anything wrong. But deep down I knew we were both living in sin. My heart knew I was fooling myself but I didn't want to let go.

I had never been cared for by someone like the way he did. He invoked feelings I never knew existed. He was the only one who made me happy. With him, I felt special; he made me feel that I was beautiful and worthy of love.

Ours was not a happily ever-after story. His behavior changed. It dawned on me that what he felt for me wasn't love but obsession. Our relationship turned into a nightmare. I was devastated thinking that I hoped for a glimpse of heaven, but what I got was a taste of hell.

I wanted to escape from his shadow so I decided to attend a youth camp. It was like fighting a battle without knowing my enemies, without any weapon at hand. I didn't know what could happen in the camp. All I desired was to get away from him for awhile.

For the first two days of the youth camp, I chose to be just a listener. When everyone started to share their struggles and darkest moments in life, I was tempted to participate but I managed to shut up because I was so afraid of their judgments. I knew I was in a sinful relationship, but hearing that from someone else was something I wasn't ready for. Not one of my closest friends knew about my situation. I kept everything in secret. My relationship was the kind I would never be able to boast of. It was something I preferred to be kept hidden from everyone.

The youth camp's culmination day came. The facilitator instructed us to let go of whatever pain, fears, anger, doubts, regrets and hatred we kept within.

I knew right there and then that it was time to share but since I wasn't comfortable to tell the group, I spoke to the facilitator privately. I never thought it was possible for me to open up to a person I hardly knew. The fear that I would be condemned vanished. So I told her everything.

Pouring my whole heart out, I narrated my story in between sobs. She didn't utter any word. Her embrace filled my heart with peace. I looked into her eyes and I saw mercy, while there was no trace of judgment on her face. She smiled and said words that lingered in my heart even up to now.

"Ada, God has forgiven you even before you ask Him for it. He loves you and no mistake you've ever made can make His love for you any less. He cares for you. You're His beautiful daughter. He doesn't look at your sin; He looks at the beauty He created in you. No matter how many times you drive him away, He will still be by your side; He will never leave you nor forsake you. Each time you stumble, He will be there to help you stand up again. Rise from where you fall. Forgive yourself as God forgives you. Love yourself as God loves you."

Her message pierced my heart. I knew I was talking to Jesus in her.

For the first time in my life, I prayed like I never prayed before. I bowed my head saying: "Father God, I'm sorry for the ways I've been living my life. I know I've got to change. Take me out of the darkness. Help me see the light of your presence and guide me to the path of righteousness."

When I went home, I prayed without ceasing. Then, I decided to talk to him.

"Let's stop this. I don't want to be with you anymore." I said with utter determination.

I saw fire in his eyes as he spoke: "If you will leave me, I will post our pictures in social media, I will tell your family and friends that you're nothing but a mistress!"

I knew he was just threatening me but somehow, it was effective. I thought of how devastated my family would feel if they would know, and I wondered if I would have any friends left. Then I thought about the kind of life I would live without him. I was used to living in luxury; he provided my needs and wants.

He was everything to me. To top it all, I had given him my all. I was in the middle of a crossroad: one to my comfort zone and one that goes to my courage zone.

Then I heard a soft whisper of a voice in my heart: "You have me Ada. I love you no matter what. I will never leave you."

God's comforting words massaged my heart and I had the courage to dump the man I thought I loved. I lost a sinful relationship and I later gained the best relationship ever: my relationship with Christ.

It was never easy to start all over again, however God sent me to a loving community, helping me to recover from my brokenness.

I started to respect my body as the temple of the Holy Spirit and I realized my true value. I remembered what Crystalina Evert said: "God is a God of second chances."

God changed my life in ways I never thought was possible. He led me out of the darkness to His light. He replaced my frustrations with His peace and the temporary happiness with His immeasurable joy.

I fully understood what it means to be under God's sufficient grace. I am now living a chaste life, utilizing my dark past as a lesson for me to move forward.

When I learned that Elly needed a story of a woman who used to have lots of insecurities but later realized that even her weaknesses can be used by God for His greater glory, I bravely messaged her: "I am that woman."

Yes, I am that woman. I didn't see my worth before. I used to live my life in the shadow of my dark past and now, God can use my story to inspire women who are still imprisoned in a sinful relationship. If I did it, you can too.

Just like my friend Ada, let go of life's uncertainties and surrender to God's perfect plans for your life. It doesn't matter where you've been or who you were before. Let your story be a living testimony that God works everything for the good of those who love Him. Don't underestimate yourself. You are special in God's eyes, and you have your own mission to fulfill.

Regardless of your bad decisions in the past, you are still worth waiting for. If you are still currently in a sinful relationship, ask God for the courage to let go.

Even if you have lost your virginity already, you still have yourself to give. You are still worth pure, authentic love from someone who is man enough to guard your purity as well as his own despite your past mistakes. But first, you need to respect yourself. Raise your standards when it comes to relationships. You don't need to be in a relationship just to feel loved. Know that whatever your status is, God loves you. God can forgive you if you already had sex outside the covenant of marriage. It's never too late to live a life of purity.

Sacred Scripture says in 1 Corinthians 7:34 "And the unmarried woman and the virgin are anxious about the affairs of the Lord, so that they may be holy in body and spirit..."

So virginity is spiritual as well as physical. So there is great hope! You can become a spiritual virgin again! But you will need to repent of any sexual encounters you have had outside the covenant of marriage. If you are Catholic you will need to go to the Sacrament of Reconciliation (Confession) and seek God's mercy, grace and forgiveness through that wonderful sacrament.

Still doubting if God has forgiven you or can forgive you of sexual immorality? Let me give you an assurance from one of my favorite stories from the Bible:

> "The teachers of the Law and the Pharisees brought in a woman who had been caught committing adultery, and they made her stand before them all. "Teacher," they said to Jesus, "this woman was caught in the very act of committing adultery. In our Law Moses commanded that such a woman must be stoned to death. Now, what do you say?" They said this to trap Jesus, so that they could accuse him. But he bent over and wrote on the ground with his finger. As they stood there asking him questions, he straightened up and said to them: "Whichever one of you has committed no sin may throw the first stone at her." Then he bent over again and wrote on the ground. When they heard this, they all left, one by one, the older ones first. Jesus was left alone, with the woman still standing there. He straightened up and said to her, "Where are they? Is there no one left to condemn you?"
>
> "No one, sir," she answered.
>
> "Well, then," Jesus said, "I do not condemn you either. Go, but sin no more."

Jesus' mercy is the same today. He doesn't look at your sin but rather focuses on the beauty that He created in you. However, His forgiveness is not a license for you to sin again. Note how Jesus said it clearly: GO, BUT SIN NO MORE.

Furthermore, let these words from Blessed Mother Teresa inspire you to live a pure life starting now:

> "The devil may try to use the hurts of life, and sometimes your own mistakes, to make you feel it is impossible that Jesus really loves you, is really cleaving to you. This is a danger for all of us. And so sad, because it is completely the opposite of what Jesus is really wanting, waiting to tell you. Not only that He loves you, but even more, He longs for you. He misses you when you don't come close. He thirsts for you. He loves you always, even when you don't feel worthy, when not accepted by others, even by yourself sometimes. He is the one who always accepts you. Only believe that you are precious to Him. Bring all your suffering to His feet, only open your heart to be loved by Him as you are. He will do the rest."

Prayer:

"Father God, thank you for forgiving me; thank you for looking at me not with judgmental eyes but with your most loving and comforting gaze. Help me forgive those who have hurt me, and help me to forgive myself. Help me not to see my past as a stumbling block but a lesson for me to keep moving forward. I offer my life to you. Here's my whole heart Father. Take it as it is, broken and full of scars. I know only you can heal me. Create in me a new heart, a heart that believes in your infinite mercy, that it's never too late to be the person you called me to be."

Live In The "Now"
© Erlita Suarez Cabal

Let your deepest wounds of yesterday,
Be your greatest gifts of today;
Don't live your life in the shadow of your past,
Happy thoughts are the ones that should last.

The past is something you cannot change,
Let go of your brokenness, break the chains!
Believe that the future looks bright;
Have faith that you are precious in God's sight.

Bid farewell to the pains of long ago,
God has a great future in store for you;
Always look beyond your flaws and imperfections,
Every pain will bring you to your mission.

Chapter 9

PEARLS OF WISDOM FOR SINGLE MOMS

"But those who trust in the Lord for help will find their strength renewed. They will rise on wings like eagles; they will run and not get weary; they will walk and not grow weak (Isaiah 40:31)."

Guest Testimonies

JOURNEY OF GREAT TORMENT AND FINALLY SURRENDER

The following testimony was written by Brendan's friend from the U.S. She courageously shares her testimony which includes great suffering, walking away from God, becoming an atheist and then her journey back. She recounts how that no matter what someone does in their life, including making selfish and horrific decisions, there is always hope because our merciful Father is always waiting for us:

I was born into a family that was Catholic in name only. We went to Mass every Sunday, often late and said grace before meals. That was about it. One of my parents would usually come into my room at night when I went to bed and say some formal prayers with me. But religion was never really discussed or put into action. My mother read religious books occasionally and sometimes I would sneak them off her bookshelf after she was done with them. My parents fought constantly. They always talked about divorce, but I got so used to it that I was sure it would never be anything more than talk.

Somehow I developed a fascination with supernatural events at a young age. Most of my reading material as a child was books about various saints and Eucharistic miracles. I used to go outside on the balcony at night and talk to God, just in case He was real. A few times I felt like I had some mystical experiences, but even if they were more than my imagination they never changed me for very long.

Growing up was a constant search for meaning in my life. I began to find it when my father was transferred to Indonesia when I was 13. I had never really believed that poverty like that could be a way of life for people and I wanted to be a missionary for a long time after we came home from there. The next year I began going to a Catholic charismatic youth group and had my first distinct experience with God at a retreat in Steubenville, Ohio. I thought nothing could shake my faith after that. But when I was 14 I began a relationship with my older brother's friend that became way too intense way too quickly.

I told him I wanted to wait until marriage, but I didn't act in accordance with that statement very much. We talked as if we were definitely going to get married right from the start, so I behaved as if everything except "the act" was ok. Then one day he told me that it had really happened that time. I was too shocked to feel betrayed. We had only been together for a few months. I felt dirtier than I thought was possible for any human to feel. By this time I had become agnostic and practically atheist, like my boyfriend, but I had a deep inner longing to be with only one person my entire life, and now it all felt empty and ruined. After that I gave up the fight.

We were together for over eight years. Things got progressively more dysfunctional; he became addicted to marijuana and pain medications, when he could find them and began to be insanely jealous and physically abusive. The last two problems were less intense over the last few years, but none of them ever really went away.

I tried to convince myself that I was happy. I built a façade of contentedness that I portrayed to everyone I knew so that they wouldn't feel sorry for me. My world would be over, I felt, if anyone ever found out how miserable I was. If this was ever discovered then my family would have "won". They would have succeeded in making me like them. The only way to rise above them, in my mind, was to prove to them that I had achieved happiness despite their dysfunctionalism, so no matter whatever happened I had to look like I had it all together. I had to show everyone that I was secure.

This was the mindset that I had when, at age 17, my period was late. I didn't even think about the possibility of being pregnant until several days had gone by, even though I was like clockwork down to the hour, because that simply couldn't happen to me. I knew the cycle. We were abstinent during the "unsafe" times, so it was just impossible. When I threw up one morning I looked at the cycle again in my Biology textbook and was horrified to find out that my understanding of the time of ovulation had been off by a week.

That afternoon I called my boyfriend crying when the home pregnancy test was positive. He came over and hugged me and took me to the abortion clinic for a "real" test. The nurse didn't tell me the results of the test when she came back up front. She just handed me a form to bring to a judge for a judicial bypass so I didn't have to tell my parents (since I was a minor).

We went to the courthouse the next day. When our appointment time came, the lawyer asked me for evidence of my maturity. I told him how I was ranked third in my class academically. When the judge asked me why I wanted to do this I explained how dysfunctional my family was and how I had my whole future planned out and this would mess everything up for me. That was enough for him. When the clerk came out to hand me the signed letter she wished me good luck.

We were late the day of the abortion. My boyfriend punched a hole in the wall that morning before pushing me across the room after I tried to rush him one too many times. We had to break through protesters outside. I remember worrying that my mother was among them. I waited all day long, from 9:30 am until 6 pm, sitting on the floor because there weren't enough chairs. I felt nothing. There was complete silence all day. People pretended to read magazines and to not hear what the protesters were saying outside.

When I went back, in the last group, there was nervous laughter after the abortion procedure was explained. In the room, I remember feeling like the paper gown they gave me to wear shouldn't be white. As I was waiting for the doctor to come in a wave of emotion crashed over me. Suddenly I couldn't bear the fact that this was the last time my child and I would ever be alone together. I began bawling as I felt the pure evil of the action I was choosing at the same time as I felt that my own selfishness and cowardice was going to prevent me from leaving, which everything good in me wanted to do. I felt God's mercy drowning my soul even as I tried to convince myself He didn't really exist and I had some sense of unfinished business taking place at that moment in my heart.

The nurse came in. The emotion suddenly evaporated. I muttered something about just being nervous as she tried to ask me if I was ok. The doctor came in and convinced me that the anesthesia would make things easier, but I think they gave me too much because the rest of the evening was like a dizzy nightmare. The pain was incredible and I could barely walk afterwards. My boyfriend accused me of faking it to get attention. I was the last patient to leave the clinic that day.

The next few months are a blur to me. The worst thing was that nothing in my life changed (except for me starting birth control pills). I wanted some kind of external confirmation that my abortion had been the best or the worst decision; I wanted some kind of real-life drama to go along with the undertow tugging at my soul, but I felt there was only silence from the universe. I remember even being ambivalent about the birth of my sister's first living child a month or so later. I felt like a geyser ready to blow, waiting for the right moment. My anger and hatred for my family increased exponentially as I mounted blame on them for not creating an environment for me in which my child could have lived with a chance at real happiness.

Soon I began to have a recurrent daydream about an episode of Ray Bradbury Theater. Every morning when I was getting ready for school the scene would replay over and over in my mind. A man living with his family in a colony on another planet sometime in the future returns home from a town meeting. His wife is waiting to hear the news from him. He tells her that all of the men in the town had the same dream as he did the night before – a horrible nightmare of people burning to death, screaming in pain. At the meeting they decided that it was a premonition of events to come that very night and they gave out cyanide pills for the parents to give their children to spare them the terrible suffering. The husband and wife discuss this situation and decide, at length, that it's a risk worth taking and they will not give either of their children the pills. Then they go to sleep.

Early the next morning the wife wakes up alone. She's overjoyed to see that they made the right decision since there was no catastrophic event that night and they would have killed their children pointlessly. She calls out her husband's name and walks through the house to find him. After looking in the kitchen and outside, a look of horror comes over her face as she goes toward the children's room. She opens the door and sees him kneeling on the floor with his chin against his chest, sleeping, with one hand touching each of his children, whose beds are about three feet apart in the room.

She calls his name in a shaking voice and he wakes up, looking around him. Then in horror he realizes that he's killed his children for nothing. He looks back at his wife, who starts screaming, with unspeakable sorrow.

After a few months I mentioned the daydream to my boyfriend. We talked for awhile and decided that I was subconsciously guilty for the abortion. I didn't have the daydream again. Pretty soon, though, I felt like writing to my unborn child and naming him or her. I started off the letter by saying how ridiculous it was that I was writing since I didn't believe in God or the afterlife. I said my family and society were guilty of killing her (I began to have a sense that the child had been a girl) since they hadn't created a world in which she would have been welcomed. I told my boyfriend later that I'd decided that if I ever got pregnant again I'd have to have the child.

Our relationship was stable throughout my first three years of college. But my parents began bitter divorce proceedings in my freshman year. I testified against my father, from whom I became estranged for several years. Another fight with my older sister around the same time caused us to stop speaking for a few years.

In my senior year, just after I had finished applying for medical school for the first time, on the evening of 13 October, 1997, I was racing home to start studying for my midterms the next day. I climbed up the ladder on the side of the balcony of my house (which I had begun using the year before so I could avoid my mother by not having to enter the front door to get to my room) and then slipped off the edge of the balcony. I fell ten feet to the ground and landed in a sitting position.

I tried to get up and found that my legs wouldn't move; my back was broken and my spinal cord had been bruised. I started screaming for help and my neighbor called 911.

I was rushed to the hospital and had a spinal fusion operation the next day. My boyfriend kept telling me that we would get through this. He helped me do my exercises every day for the first few months, so I believed him.

My father and sister tried to reconcile with me, and I reluctantly began talking to them again. The physical therapy was very painful, but I kept believing that I was going to walk again someday (I still believe that). They made braces for me that allowed me to walk with crutches, but fatigue and incontinence kept me from using them as often as I wanted.

My boyfriend began coming around gradually less often, especially as I took 25 hours of classes the next semester in college so that I could graduate with my class since I was still optimistic that I would get into medical school that year. A few times that spring, at my brother's request, I went to talk to the father of one of his friends outside a church during an evening prayer meeting. The last time, right after Easter, this person convinced me to go to confession (and communion), but I didn't remember about the abortion until I was trying to sleep later that night.

Soon after, I found out that I hadn't gotten into medical school and my boyfriend told me that he was leaving me for another woman, his friend's girlfriend, who he had been cheating with for the last few months. I didn't feel like I wanted to die because to myself I already felt dead. I tried in vain to hide what had happened from my family. He had alienated me from all of my friends throughout the years, so I was absolutely alone.

Thinking back I tried to remember if there was ever a time that I had experienced anything resembling happiness, and I remembered the retreat I had gone on as a freshman in High School with the charismatic youth group. It was usually in June, so I asked my cousin about going with me. He and I drove behind the buses with the other participants to Steubenville. We talked about religion on the way. I told him about the abortion and decided to confess it when we got there.

I opened myself up to the possibility that God might exist. Because of my curiosity in this regard, and because of a cute youth leader I had met at the retreat, I began going to the weekly meetings of the charismatic organization. The guy I liked went to daily Mass, so I started going too. Gradually my soul was opening up to this new life. I read a book called *The Way of a Pilgrim* about a Russian peasant on a mission to learn how to pray constantly, and all of a sudden I believed. I had been refusing the Eucharist at Mass up to this point because I didn't believe in the Real Presence, but now I didn't just want it, I needed it. I began going to Mass multiple times some days. I attended a different prayer meeting every night and went to hear every speaker at every church. I went to Eucharistic adoration and read any religious book I could get my hands on. My relationship with my family improved as I prayed for the grace to forgive both them and myself.

In December, 1998 I went to see *The Prince of Egypt* at the movie theater. Something stirred in my soul as I watched, but I wasn't sure what. That night, as I was pulling out of the driveway of my house for the last time (I was moving into my own apartment thanks to my disability check), a song came on the Christian radio station. I still don't know what it was called, but the woman was asking God why He had created her instead of somebody wiser or better. All of a sudden emotion overtook me. It felt almost like the continuation of the sadness I had been overwhelmed with on the operating table in the abortion clinic. Now I knew what had struck me so deeply about the movie – Moses' mother had risked her life to save her son from Pharaoh's soldiers. Not only had I not risked my life for my child, I had paid someone to kill her just for the sake of my own convenience. How could I ever live with myself? How could I live in the joy of Christ when I was constantly remembering that I was a murderer in the back of my mind?

That night I cried for almost four hours. A few days later when I saw the leader I liked in the youth group, who I'd become friends with, I told him I needed to talk to him. He told me he'd woken up a few nights before feeling like he needed to tell me about God's mercy. When I probed further I discovered he'd woken up at the exact moment I'd started crying that night! We talked later that week and I asked him why I should try to go to Heaven when I deserved Hell. He told me "Because Jesus wants you there".

After a few days, at his urging, I called a Crisis Pregnancy Center and offered my services as a volunteer counselor. It was very rewarding talking to the women on the phone, although very few of them seemed to listen to what I had to say; I was only able to convince one young lady to keep her child. My story found its way to the leaders of my youth group, though, and they asked me to share my testimony with 5,000 participants at the Southern Regional Conference of the Catholic Charismatic Renewal. My parents came, and it was the first time they heard about the abortion.

In the fall of that same year, 1999, I began medical school in Nashville, Tennessee at the only place that had accepted me after my second round of applying. It was and still is a struggle to find a balance between my desire for spiritual growth and the numerous demands on my time. But God willing I still hope to become as holy as God intends by the time I'm on my deathbed.

I feel that my calling is to work for the pro-life movement in New York City, which has one of the highest abortion rates in the world, and to have a very large family that trusts completely in God's providence. I still have to forgive myself anew every day for the child I aborted and the children that were probable victims of the abortifacient birth control pills I was on for five years. I have to be careful that Satan doesn't make me feel unworthy to spread the Good News or entice me to think prideful thoughts. I seek frequent strength from confession and the Eucharist and look forward to sharing a deep spiritual life with my future husband and family and living for all eternity with the awesome God who stretched out His hand to save me from Hell! Please pray for me that I may help do as much for others as He has done for me!

I Choose To Live
© Brendan Roberts

I hear your voices;
There are words of pain;
And words of love.

Today mummy I felt you running;
And Daddy, urging you to go faster.
Then Daddy talked about the field;
Mummy was excited about its beauty.
I want to see!

Now Mummy and Daddy are arguing;
They say they have to make a choice;
That they won't have enough money.
Money seems more important than me;
I'm so depressed!
But, oh how I want to live!

Mummy I'm so happy;
When I feel your body,
Rising and lifting with joy;
But your laughter has vanished.

Now your body is in spasms;
Your anguish over the decision,
Tears me apart.
But Mummy I'll help you;
I choose to live!

Mourning Turned To Dancing

Vanessa, a good friend of mine way back in college, shared to me the sufferings and joys of being a single mom:

When infatuation brought me to an unwanted pregnancy, I thought abortion was the solution. But praise God for all the good friends around. They never failed to remind me that every child is a blessing and that God will provide.

I was a coward. I was afraid of life's uncertainties. I wasn't ready to let go of my personal ambition. I cared too much about other people's opinion of me more than my soul. But finally my kind spirit knocked me off as friends stayed by my side all the time. They made me realize that I've sinned but I'm already forgiven. Together we fought and won! And I never regret to have known them for I have possessed the brightest jewel of my life: my son!

What makes a woman a "superwoman"? It is to dwell in one human body but having the spirit of both man and a woman. Being a single mom at 24, I am both a mother and a father to my 3-year old son. I constantly manage my time to perform a dual role. I am a provider. I spend sleepless nights to work hard for all his needs. I am the protector.

I conquer my fears to make him safe. I plan for his bright future every minute of the day. I take care of the household chores. I cook. I wash all his dirty clothes. I teach him the ABC's. I go out and play with him though I'm tired from work. I sing a lullaby every night to make him sleep. I give him my warmest hugs and kisses.

I do all these things day by day but I will never stop. I admit it's never easy but I am not giving up for God knows where I'm heading and He's leading the way.

For all single moms out there, I hope we share the same happiness and hopes. Let's continue to love our children unconditionally. But we must not forget ourselves as well. Be who you want to be and make your child your inspiration. Women like us are empowered. We are very blessed!

I pray that the testimonies touched your heart.

If you have aborted your child, run to the Sacrament of Reconciliation and surrender all your sins to God. He has been patiently waiting for you to run to Him. Meet God halfway. Repent and live a new life.

If you got pregnant out of wedlock and you're planning to get rid of your child, please remember that the life in your womb is the greatest gift of womanhood. Keep your child for every child is a miracle.

Not all women are given the precious gift of motherhood. While you are planning to abort your child, many women out there are praying to have one. There are those who have had miscarriages and are still longing to have children.

Each time you get tired of juggling too many things, always look up to Jesus; His wisdom surpasses any parenting books available. He makes a perfect husband too. Surrender your heart completely to God. Concentrate on becoming the best parent to your child.

Don't think that God loves you any less than your married or single friends. God loves you the same. Never think that just because you stumbled, you're no longer worthy of love. Believe that a man will truly love you and will accept your child as his own if it's God's will.

If someone pursues you, always consider your child's welfare before committing to a relationship. What's good for your child must be your utmost priority; a crucial part of every decision you will make in your life.

Fix your eyes on God and in providing a brighter future for your child. Take care of yourself and continue to reach for your dreams in life. You can still be who you want to be. Never lose hope.

Prayer:

"Father God, thank you for forgiving my sins. I surrender my whole life to you. Help me to live life anew. Please grant me the grace to always live in hope, peace, faith and love."

I Love You Mommy
© Erlita Suarez Cabal

Thank you for loving me even before I was born,
I felt your love even from the depths of your womb;
I was enveloped in God's sufficient grace,
When I felt your first embrace…

When I look into your eyes, I see love;
Truly you are a gift from up above,
Your delicate touch brings healing;
Mommy, you are my everything!

Chapter 10

HE LOVES ME, HE LOVES ME NOT?

"Love never gives up; and its faith, hope, and patience never fail (1 Corinthians 13:7).

Have you tried pulling off petals from a flower in your hopes to find out if a guy really loves you? I remember doing that when I was a teenager and was head over heels in love with a basketball player back in my hometown. I caught him looking at me during basketball games (Maybe he was only looking at me because I was the scorer! Haha). So by the time I went home, I searched through my mother's garden and pulled out some yellow blooms. If the last petal matched the words "He loves me not" I would grab another flower until the last petal matched the words "He loves me."

That didn't work of course. Instead of the cute basketball player pursuing me, I found myself running as fast as I could while my mother chased after me with a witch's broom in her hand, extremely agitated that I ruined her precious garden.

You may not be pulling out a flower's petal now but I know you've asked this question: "How do I know if he really loves me?" You might have asked this question when you started going out with a man who showed interest in you or maybe when you're already in a relationship.

One lazy afternoon, I opened my browser and typed on Google: "How do I know if a man really loves me?'

Google provided the following links:

- 17 Signs He is in Love with You
- "Does He Love Me" Quiz
- Biggest Signs that He is in Love with You
- 20 Sure Signs to Read His Mind
- 7 Signs He Knows the Definition of Love
- 10 Signs that He Loves Me

Well, I had fun browsing the results but something was lacking. None of the results quenched my thirst for the perfect answer.

Contrary to what you might be expecting, I won't give you a list of signs to know if a man really loves you. I'm not providing you a quiz to measure a man's love either. But hey! Don't close the book just yet. I have one answer to that question. Yeah, not many, just one.

Are you ready for my answer? Signs are not even needed.

No need to answer a quiz. How do you know if a man really loves you?

Here's the answer: [Note from Brendan: Finally!!!!]

HE LEADS YOU CLOSER TO GOD.

Yes, you read it right. A man who truly loves you is concerned about getting your soul to heaven. Therefore, he will not lead you into sin. He will not take your time off from God. He will journey with you in faith instead.

HE LEADS YOU CLOSER TO GOD. Just that, only one statement, yet everything springs forth from it.

When you're already in a relationship, it's easier to figure out if the man really loves you. Allow me to elaborate further by asking you these questions: (Kindly ponder your answers in your heart):

Do you pray together?

In prayer, you share an intimacy founded on a solid rock: Jesus Christ. I heard couples say that a strong bond of intimacy can be achieved through sex. This is true between married couples. In the act of making love, you are proclaiming: "I'm all yours". Now if you're doing it outside marriage, you can say: "I'm all yours" but that's gonna be a lie. Just because you two are in a relationship doesn't give both of you a license to own each other's body.

If you really want to create a strong bond, then prayer is the best antidote. Once the relationship is centered in Christ, the stronger the foundation is for marriage. I know a couple who prays together. They have daily prayer dates. Together, they thank God for daily blessings and miracles, they pray for each other's struggles and not just that, they intercede for other people. In fact, they are my prayer warriors. What a better world it will be if all couples do the same! Praying together will equip the couple to be the best parents, passing on the beauty of prayer to their children.

I'm not saying you should break up with your boyfriend right away because you two are not praying together. I encourage you to start praying together now. Make it a habit. You will be amazed once you start doing it. Through prayer dates, it would be easier for you both to combat the struggles within the relationship.

Are you losing your identity in the process?
Your man should understand that he is a part of your world, but not all of it. I have a friend who's afraid to follow her dreams in life for she might lose her boyfriend in the process. She shared how much she wanted to go abroad but was just too scared that another woman will snatch her boyfriend away from her. My friend chose to stay because she doubted if long distance relationships work. I told her that a relationship must be founded on trust and not on fears.

A man who truly loves you will support your God-given dreams. He will inspire and encourage you to be the woman God has always wanted you to be, be it together or apart.

Likewise ladies, if your man wants to pursue his passion in life, support him and pray with him. Bring out the best in him.

Does he treat you with respect?
I'm not just referring to opening the car door for you, pulling out a chair for you to sit on at your dinner date in a restaurant, or taking you home safely. Although those gentlemanly actions really melt a woman's heart, respect is way more than that. How does he deal with conflicts and misunderstandings? Does he hurt you emotionally, spiritually or physically? I remembered seeing bruises on my colleague's arm; I asked her what happened and her answer shocked me to my core: "My boyfriend hit me; we had a fight this morning because he was jealous. But that's okay, I understand him; he loves me too much that he's afraid to lose me. I'm used to it".

I was like, "What?!"

Ladies, don't mistake possessiveness with love. Respect has all to do with how he treats your body. Sure, he has sexual desires but remember that you're not an object to be conquered but a treasure to be cherished. Don't mistake obsession with love.

Notice how he treats the women in his life, like his mom, sisters, and friends. The way he treats other women will somehow affect how he will treat you in the future.

Ladies, respect your man as well. Don't forget that he is a child of God. He is God's prince, so treat him as such. Assist him in guarding your purity as well as his own. Don't use your charm or your body to lure both of you into sin. Beauty is power, use it well.

Prayer:

"Father God, thank you for showing us what perfect love is. Help us build a relationship centered in you; a relationship based on love and not on lust. Help us honor you in our relationship; make it holy and pleasing to you. Amen."

Now And Hereafter
© Erlita Suarez Cabal

This love I offer you,
No one can love you like I do;
You are worthy of My blood,
I'll do everything to make you glad...

I'll be here,
Loving you beyond forever;
Now and hereafter,
I'll be right here...

Surrender your heart to me,
Let surprises come your way;
Trust in me, I trust in you,
Together, we will build a love so true...

Chapter 11

WALK ON WATER

"I can do all things through Christ who strengthens me (Philippians 4:13)."

"Just one little step Elly and you'll be all right! Common! Just one leap of faith!"

Rousha, my spiritual sister at work, shook my shoulder and spoke these words with authority. I was seated helplessly on the floor, weeping, my gaze focused on my trembling hands.

"I can't! I'm so damn afraid!" I answered in between sobs.

"Just say YES!" Her jaws tightened. Every inch of her wanted to pull me out from the walls of fear I had built around me. Her heart was moved with pity. She held my face and gently told me: "You are designed for greatness Elly; God has a beautiful purpose for your life. Use your gift now to bless the world." Just that and my mind were filled with memories as to how it all begun...

My dilemma started when I attended a talk entitled "Fabulous Midlife Madness" sponsored by a women's Catholic organization called JEWELS (J-esus in E-very W-oman E-mpowered to L-ove and S-erve). The speaker was Ditas Espanol, the head of Light of Jesus Counseling Ministry. I felt a pinch in my heart when she said: "Be sensitive to where God is calling you." I felt something strange deep within me, a feeling I couldn't even describe in words. I had goose bumps! I knew God wanted to tell me something very important, but I brushed off that feeling.

God spoke to me again through a priest when I served as Sunday school teacher in *Awesome Kids Ministry* at Feast Greenhills. The Gospel was about Peter walking on water. It seemed like the priest looked at me in the eyes when he said: "Walking on water is going beyond your personal limitations, beyond your fears." The message pierced my heart.

Those messages haunted me for so many nights that I could no longer sleep properly.

"When you feel like you're not ready, GOD IS READY", is a third message God sent me through a friend's Facebook post (Wow! God talked to me even on Facebook!) God was so clear in giving me messages; He even sent messages through billboards, flyers, and even quotes printed on the t-shirts of those people who passed me by.

What was stopping me from obeying God? It was fear, fear of the unknown, the blade of uncertainty that stabbed my heart.

One glorious Wednesday night, on bended knees, I prayed to God: "Father, I believe you have great plans for me but I still don't know which way to go, I'm having a hard time discerning; lead me to where you want me to be. Create in me a brave heart that follows your most holy will. Direct my path Father. I don't want to do things on my own anymore; I don't want to get ahead of your plans. Teach me to place my trust in you alone. Here is my life. I surrender my all to you. Take me as I am. Help me become the person you always wanted me to be. Grant me the gift of obedience to follow whatever you would tell me to do. Take the wheel of my life Father. Take over…take over…Father, I can't take this anymore, please speak to me now. What do you want me to do?"

After I uttered that prayer, God prompted me to open His love letters for me, the ones sent from GodWhispers.com. I've written all the letters in my spiritual journal. God told me that the first letter is His message for me. Lo and behold, when I opened my journal, I saw this letter:

Dear Elly,

Go to where you're appreciated, not to where you're tolerated. I have given you gifts; don't throw them to the swine.
I believe in you,

God.
P.S. Waiting for your go signal to bless you even more.

I cried after reading the letter. God was so specific. He wanted me to get out from my comfort zone. The battle was within me.

Most often than not, I ask for God's assurances first before I obey Him. What He asked of me was to walk on water blindfolded, tossed by the strong winds and gigantic waves.

Even after reading that letter, I didn't find the courage to let go of my fears. I was so afraid that if I gave up my job, I wouldn't be able to pay for my sister's tuition fee anymore. Added to that, my mother called me and said she had a dream that we live in a tiny house; that we're so busy repairing it for in no time, the house would collapse. That didn't do any good to my already troubled heart.

We've been through that and I don't want it to happen again. When I was 16, I even had to work as an all-around maid. I had to bear the load of juggling the household chores and taking care of a two-year-old baby girl. My situation was tearing me up inside but that was the only way then for me to finish college. My goal was to find work right away to support my younger sister's studies.

No matter how much I wanted to venture on writing right after my graduation, I didn't as I knew for starters that the income wouldn't be enough to help fund my sister. I rolled up my sleeves in the corporate world out of love for my sister; I didn't want her to experience all the hardships I went through.

I had so many questions. My heart was deeply troubled; full of doubts and fears. However, God was so patient with me. He brought me to the Prayer and Life workshop at St Francis Church. The topic was "Mother Mary's Obedience to God's Will for Her life." I was amazed at Mother Mary's reply when an angel appeared to tell her she will conceive the Messiah. Full of humility and trust in the Father, she replied: "I am the Lord's servant, may it be done to me according to your word."

"Why can't I be like Mother Mary?" This was the cry of my heart.

If I was Mother Mary then and was told the same thing that the angel told her, my answer could have been too far from Mother Mary's humble reply. I could have answered: "Hello! Are you kidding me? What would people think about me if I get pregnant without a husband? I don't want to be stoned to death!" or I could have said: "Why me? I'm just a poor, ordinary woman, why don't you choose a Queen?"

You see, aside from the fears I kept within, I was imprisoned in my insecurities too. I thought that I was of little value; that I could not make any difference in the world. For many years, I believed that I am nobody, that I could not do anything great.

I was lost in deep thoughts when the facilitator called me: "Elly, do you want to share something about obedience to God?" I simply answered: "I pray that I will have a heart like Mary, that I may follow God's will without questions but in total surrender." The prayer and life workshop continued smoothly and before I knew it, I was already sobbing upon hearing, "THY WILL BE DONE" not only once but six times! I was drowning in the ocean of God's leading to follow His divine purpose for my life. The facilitator noticed the emotional struggle written all over my face so she asked me again to share. To their surprise, I declared: "I will resign on Monday." That was Thursday night.

It has been my childhood dream to become a writer but as the bread winner and having the responsibility of sending my younger sister to college I had to place that dream on the backseat. Until one day, God asked me to give up my corporate job and chase after my real dream, His dream for my life.

Indeed, it is God who put that dream in my heart and He has anointed the day He will bring it into completion. I had to give up the job that had sustained me in paying my sister's tuition fee! I cried for a week; I had so many questions.

My close friend, Mitch decided to bring me to Edsa Shrine adoration chapel. She was the one who was always there as I fought my internal battles. The church was already closed so we settled outside, behind the glass windows where we could still see the Holy Eucharist.

Painted on the church's wall was a group of men listening to the radio. I noticed that on that painting, there was a little boy seated under the table, hugging the man's leg. He looked neglected. I suddenly pictured myself as part of the painting. What I saw brought me to tears. I saw myself with the little boy seated on my lap; I was stroking his hair and caressing his back while talking to him with eyes full of compassion and love.

Through that vision, God made me realize that He has given me the gift of kindness, not just through my actions but through the gift of kind words.

Mitch suddenly approached me, holding a Bible in her hand she told me: "God asked me to give you His message, He wants you to read 1 Corinthians 7:17. Here's my Bible, open it."

With trembling hands, I opened the Bible and looked for the verse Mitch gave me. I shed buckets of tears as I read: *"Each of you should go on living according to the Lord's gift to you, and as you were when God called you."*

God's message was as clear as the sun at midday.

I resigned from my corporate job, the job that had sustained me in paying my sister's tuition fee and in helping my family. I was overwhelmed at the many gifts and messages I got from my officemates. I never thought I had touched their lives. My resignation became an instrument for them to seek God's divine purpose for their lives as well.

Days passed after my resignation and it felt like a journey to the great unknown, yet, with a great leap of faith and with the prayers of the people around me, I declared: "THY WILL BE DONE! I'm happy to tell you that the Lord is faithful, He fulfills His promises; I felt blessed like never before when I obeyed Him and surrendered my life to Him.

I am so blessed being surrounded with people who kept on pushing me towards reaching my dreams.

Brandon, my spiritual brother, never fails to remind me to be the woman God wants me to be. He pushed me into believing that I am capable of reaching my dreams.

Hassie, my spiritual sister at The Feast, Ortigas (a Catholic prayer meeting of the Light of Jesus family) saw a vision of me launching my first book. She was the same person who told me that she felt I will be featured in Kerygma Magazine (an inspirational magazine published by Shepherd's Voice Publications) and it did happen!

I was featured in November 2013 issue of Kerygma Magazine which was read by a film maker who later offered a huge writing project for me. I'll be the story writer of a movie that will be produced soon. Truly, God is a God of surprises! I thank God for His sufficient grace. He equipped me with an armor of faith which fuels me to reach the deepest desire He placed in my heart.

Surprises kept on coming my way. When I prayed for a mentor in my writing career, God sent Brendan Roberts (a Catholic missionary and author from New Zealand) the same day I uttered that prayer. God led him to St Francis adoration chapel where he saw me reading my journal. Since then, a God-centered friendship blossomed and we're now helping each other in accomplishing the mission God has set for us.

As of writing, it has been 6 months since I resigned from my job and embraced the life of a freelance writer. God has been faithful. He has opened doors of opportunities I never thought were possible. Truly, God opens doors that no one can shut and shuts doors that no one can open.

Now, I urge you to pray big prayers and watch God do the impossible! Don't use your energy to worry, use your energy to believe. Life is short; the perfect moment to focus on your passion is NOW.

Do the things that you love doing and offer everything to God. Don't be afraid to step out of your boat and walk on water, as long as you fix your eyes on Jesus, you will cross the other shore of your dreams safe and sound. Allow God to control your life. He has a beautiful plan for your life. You are created for a beautiful purpose. Just do it! Surrender your life to Him and declare: "THY WILL BE DONE"

Prayer:

"Father God, thank you for my talents. Help me use every gift you blessed me with to glorify you and build your kingdom here on earth. Remove the fears, doubts, and inhibitions in my heart. Replace it with your peace and love. Please grant me the courage to step out of my comfort zone and reach the edge of the great unknown. I know Father that you will be with me, you will hold my hands and you will guide my feet as I walk on water with you. Amen"

Persevere!
© Erlita Suarez Cabal

Sometimes things can go wrong,
So better learn to be strong;
Don't forget the beauty of your smile,
After having countless deep sighs.

When everything feels like uphill struggle,
Rise each time you stumble and fall;
The road to success is rough,
So you better learn how to be tough!

Your heart may be full of wounds,
That's life, full of twists and turns!
Life gives us many reasons to cry,
But God gives us countless reasons to smile!

In the midst of sacrifices and doubts,
Learn to laugh, not to pout;
A quitter never wins and a winner never quits,
It's when things seem worst that you must not quit!

Chapter 12

JOY IN THE MIDST OF PAIN

"Consider it pure joy my brothers, whenever you face trials of many kinds, because you know that the testing of your faith develops perseverance (James 1:2-3)."

What sad occurrence weighs on your heart today? Are you suffering right now? If so, then be grateful because you can turn your wounds into wisdom!

I was led to sacrifice at a young age. It wasn't because I have irresponsible parents. My brother got hospitalized and we incurred huge hospital bills. I tried to apply to fastfood chains and supermarkets but being a minor, I was turned down so I ended up working as a baby sitter and an all-round maid when I was 16 to help my parents pay off their debts.

I worked during summer vacations when I entered university. When I was in first year college, I worked as a cashier in the supermarket during summer breaks. It was so tiring having to stand 8 hours a day, and to top it all, I had to pack extremely heavy grocery items like liquor and huge canned goods just for a small amount of salary. It was hard to sleep well at night as my body ached from the previous day's hard toil. I had fever on my third day at work and it was difficult for me to move but I managed to endure the pain.

When I was in second year college, I worked as a house helper during our summer break to pay for the next semester. It was really tough! I was the only helper serving a couple and their four kids aged 1, 5, 8, and 11. It was then that I learned the art of multitasking. I did 5 errands at the same time. While food was being cooked, I washed a mountain of dirty clothes with my hands, not with a washing machine! Then I mopped the floor, bathed the 5 year old while occasionally running to the 1 year old each time she'd cry for milk.

There were many times that I wanted to give up but I didn't for I knew in my heart I was doing it not for myself but for my family. At first, I didn't understand why I had to go through a series of challenges which at my young age were too hard to bear. When I was asked to deliver a speech during our college graduation for the Tribute to Parents Ceremony, I understood that God used me to inspire others; to be a living testimony that poverty is not a hindrance to success. In my speech, I shared how I skipped meals just so I could buy materials for my projects. Studying with an empty stomach wasn't that easy but I chose to focus on the brighter side of things than living my life in agony. Admittedly though, there were times I envied other students who were born with a silver spoon in their mouth but I chose to focus more on what I could do and left the things I didn't have control over. I held onto the promise I made to my father that once I finished college, I would be the one to support my younger sister's college education. Through God's grace, I was able to fulfill that promise.

That wasn't the end of my sufferings.

I was already working when my heart was filled with grief too deep for words upon knowing that I lost my first degree cousin. Suicide was the cause of her death.

The pain was unbearable as the sad news arrived while I was still mending my broken heart caused by a man whom was never mine and will never be. I had been receiving heartbreak after heartbreak. First one was brought by a failed love story that had started to grow as a tiny bud but did not even blossom to a beautiful fragrant rose. Second was caused by a sudden death of a loved one.

As you can see I've been through a lot. If I would be asked to rate the pain from 1 to 10, that was definitely a 10. I wasn't sure if my heart was strong enough to handle everything. Every inch of my being was dying; every part had been crushed to tiny pieces.

That very moment when I wanted to weep like a little child, my DGROUP family (A Christian discipleship group of single women) surprised me with a birthday cake, a giant birthday card, a beautifully wrapped gift in pink tied with gold ribbon, and a fairy head dress. As they sang "Happy Birthday", I felt God telling me: "My daughter, your sorrow is temporary. Look! I have a surprise for you!"

Instead of questioning God as to why He allowed such deep pain to creep into my whole being, I chose to still praise Him.

Two months after my first degree cousin's death, another first degree cousin of mine died. It was a tragic death. He was stabbed to death and the painful thing was, the criminal escaped. That happened when I was also facing financial struggles. I felt so weak I cried rivers of tears.

I don't know the pains you had in the past nor the sorrows you have today. Maybe you also suffered loss of a loved one; someone might have wronged you a few years back; the person you love might have dumped you for someone else; your boss might have humiliated you in front of others; your parents might have hurt you emotionally and physically; or your friends might have forsaken you at times when you needed them the most. From the smallest to the biggest things that caused you suffering, decide to let go and let God heal the pain.

Failure to let go of past heartaches and holding onto grudges and anger will only cause harm to your life. Trials are the proof of how strong you are. Don't let the pain destroy you, use that pain instead as a stepping stone towards overcoming your Goliaths and walk out from the prison of past pains triumphantly.

Allow your pain to mold you and use your pain to bless others. Comfort those people who are experiencing the same pain you had before. Set yourself free. Life provides you with many options: Go on or give up, hold on or let go, stay or leave.

God is faithful. When God is in your heart, you can live a fulfilling life. Walk in His ways and you will truly appreciate all the days He gives you, including those painful days.

When you know your life is safe in the hands of God and that this physical life is just the beginning of eternity, then you will realize how desperately you need God and how God is faithful far beyond your desperation. Offer your life to Him in fresh gratitude. Life on earth doesn't go on forever. Find new passion to delight in the gifts of each and every day, and take none of them for granted.

Worry will not lessen your sorrow; it will only suck out the joy that today brings. Anxiety only results in wrinkles, while putting your confidence in God gives your face a natural glow!

Don't stay in the valley of tears. Soak yourself in God's ocean of mercy. God cares for you so much. He is always watching, coaching and offering encouragement at the right time.

Joy in the Midst of Pain

God's love touches your life during your darkest moments. If you have the patience to wait and see, your sorrow will be turned to joy. Remember that God listens to every silent soul prayer with empathy and love. Don't fret about so many things in life to the point of thinking that Jesus doesn't care.

Be happy now. Suffering is a gift and pain is essential. Growing up is all about getting hurt and getting over it. Pain passes away but it never leaves you empty; it will always leave you changed, wiser and stronger and it leaves a mark in your heart.

There is joy in suffering if you suffer out of love. Every time you feel pain, you need to add more love. Your suffering is your way to proclaim the presence of God. It is essential for you so you could express your presence in the sufferings of others. You can give more love to those who suffer if you've gone through a lot yourself. Through pain, you will have the wisdom to understand other people's sentiments.

Everything is passing; to worry excessively isn't healthy. Surrender everything to the Lord. There's nothing you can't handle because God is in you.

At the Cross, in the midst of pain and suffering, Jesus did not condemn those who crucified Him. Instead, full of mercy and compassion He said: "Father, forgive them, for they do not know what they do." Following Jesus' example is easier said than done. Walking with Jesus doesn't mean you will no longer stumble, it means falling over and over and over again but having the courage to stand and bounce back amidst the rocky paths of life.

You have to make spending time with God your priority. The more you pray, the stronger you become to face life's adversities.

Happiness is a choice and there's no happier life than living it for God and for others.

Prayer:

"Merciful Father, thank you for all the trials, sufferings, and pain. Thank you for always holding my hand amidst the sorrows in my life. Help me use my pain to bless others who are in dire need of comfort. Help me fix my eyes on you during the darkest moments of my life. Amen."

Wounded Healer
© Erlita Suarez Cabal

In the midst of my despair,
I breathed and I felt you in the air;
I looked up to the sky,
And the clouds proclaimed your great love.
I cried buckets of tears,
You were in my pillow where my tears fell;
I ran as fast as I could,
But you were waiting even when I was far off from the road.

Oh Lord, your presence never fails me,
In the darkness you are my light;
In my sorrow you are my joy,
You wiped the tears from my eyes.

I will finish the race for you are with me,
A wounded healer, yes I will be;
You are in me and I am in you,
I am your child, I belong to you.

Chapter 13

GLIMPSE OF HEAVEN

"Delight yourself in the Lord and He will give you the desires of your heart (Psalm 37:4)."

"How did I end up here?" The question popped in my head as soon as I reached Soekarno Hatta Airport. It all started with a tiny seed of a dream in my heart.

I'll never forget the day when I wrote on my prayer envelope: "Send me to places where You are most needed."

A few weeks after that, a friend invited me to join a mission trip to Jakarta Indonesia. I had goosebumps for I felt in my heart that it was an answered prayer. At first, it seemed impossible for I knew the trip would cost a lot.

I believe in everyday miracles. Just when I was about to give up that dream of traveling abroad for the first time, a friend approached me and asked:"How are your finances for the mission trip?" I answered, "Well, I'm still saving up for it; I still have two months." With a brilliant smile on her face, she told me:"You know what, I don't understand but God is telling me to help you. What can I do but obey?" I was totally speechless! All I did was held her hand, telling her how grateful I was.

A few days later, another friend called me up and told me she will visit me in my dormitory. I was surprised when she handed me a brown envelope with the money from her hard toil inside. Holding back the tears, I asked her why she did it, knowing that she also needed the money for her own daily expenses for just like me, she was also living independently, helping her family and working on her own. I totally lost my words when she told me: "You are a blessing to me, and I am helping you get there for I know you will be a blessing to everyone you will meet in Indonesia."

Developing a grateful heart in all circumstances has brought me to places. I saw this providence as a miracle.

With fire burning in my heart, I prepared for the mission trip. It was a social project of *Kalinangan Youth Foundation*, a study center in the Philippines. There were 11 Filipina volunteers for the cultural exchange and English Enhancement Program for high school students in Jakarta Indonesia. Our main task was to present the Philippine culture and at the same time, enhance the students' English language skills.

I was tasked to deliver a talk on Philippine Tourism. Preparing for my PowerPoint presentation on the said topic made me feel like traveling to the 17 Regions of the Philippines. I was just in front of my computer physically but my spirit for adventure and passion for travel writing pulled me out from where I was, taking me to beautiful places I'd never been.

If not for this mission trip, I wouldn't realize how beautiful my country is. Philippines is indeed a place of color and excitement! I was taken to the sights of palm-fringed white sand beaches, undulating valleys, mist-filled mountains, virgin forests, azure waters, verdant jungles, pristine waterfalls, mystical caves and vast agricultural lands. Then we should not forget the architecture and culture such as the Spanish-colonial churches, Chinese temples, Muslim mosques, and different people living in harmony. Medieval churches stand not only as architectural masterpieces, but witness to a dramatically beautiful history.

Indeed, nothing can encompass nature's prowess. The Philippines is hemmed by emerald mountains clad in dense wilderness, ragged coastline lapped by turquoise waters, bountiful pastoral lands, gorgeous waterfalls running from rainforests and stunning cave formations.

At the end of my talk, after discussing the different regions of the Philippines and what they are known for, I asked the Indonesian students to guess what the most beautiful spot in the Philippines was. The students mentioned their favorite place based on the pictures I'd shown, yet none of them gave the correct answer. With a genuine smile, I proudly said: "The most beautiful spot in the Philippines is its people; we are a bunch of happy people with friendly nature!" Their loud applause confirmed their agreement.

Gemma Galera, the mission trip organizer gave us one day to explore Indonesia's beauty. We had a tour at a place called *Taman Mini Indonesia Indah*, (Beautiful Indonesia Miniature Park). It is a culture-based recreational area located in East Jakarta, Indonesia. The park is a synopsis of Indonesian culture, with virtually all aspects of daily life in Indonesia's provinces encapsulated in separate pavilions with the collections of Indonesian architecture, clothing, dances and traditions all depicted impeccably. Apart from that, there is a lake with a miniature of the archipelago in the middle of it, cable cars, museums, *Keong Emas Imax Cinema*, a theater called *Theatre of My Homeland* (Theater Tanah Airku) and other recreational facilities.

The first experience I had was riding on the cable car with my new friends. A lively Indonesian song was playing and we danced inside the cable car. We filled our eyes with wonders. I closed my eyes as the cool wind stroked my cheek. I felt a mixture of complete joy, peace and contentment. I conquered my fear of heights! I realized that fear had played a very important role in my growth as a person. I felt the fear but I did it anyway. Had I allowed myself to surrender to my fears, I could have missed the chance to experience flying on wings of hope.

The happiness in my heart was so strong, I even felt the beating of my heart. As I looked at the beautiful scenery before my very eyes, I remembered all the people who had made my mission trip possible. In my heart I said a prayer of thanks, for I knew if it were not for them, savoring this once in a lifetime experience could have remained an elusive dream.

My face was painted with a genuine smile as I alighted from the cable car. I wasn't able to contain my excitement as we proceeded to the traditional Indonesian houses. I took a photo of myself in a traditional Indonesian wedding set. My long, flower-printed dress blended with the romantic ambiance of the place. I imagined myself seated with my prince charming as we held hands waiting for the wedding ceremony to start. Indonesia had captured my hopeless romantic heart. It awakened my desire to live a happily ever after with my prince which reminded me of what I told my single, broken-hearted friend: "Your prince charming will surely come; he may not be riding on a white horse or have his own castle, but he will love you and you alone and that's more than a fairy tale with a happily ever after!"

I enjoyed every moment as we visited the different traditional houses. The pavilions were supplemented with ornaments and motifs from each territory. They were also equipped with traditional furniture that is unique to each territory.

My favorite place was *Museum Indonesia*. A statue of a huge bird which seemed like a counterpart of the Philippines' National Eagle caught my attention. The tour guide explained that it shows Indonesia's love for unity in diversity; that people can still help each other despite speaking different languages and that the spirit of unity emerges above anything else.

We also visited Indonesia's famous bird park where I had the chance to explore the beauty of nature and be amazed with the sight of birds in different species.

Getting to *Taman Mini Indonesia Indah* was like visiting the whole Indonesia in a day, literally, because it is where the miniature of Indonesian Archipelago right in the center of its cultural sites is found. Each site represents a different part and culture from different tribes in Indonesia.

After I visited the place, I had an instant knowledge about Indonesian people, geography and even a bit of history.

Tired from the tour, we stopped for awhile and settled in one of the restaurants nearby. I love Indonesian foods! Nasi Goreng (seafood fried rice famous in Indonesia) became my favorite! It has a remarkable taste which left me craving for more! It was also in Indonesia that I discovered my love for green tea ice cream!

My beautiful journey didn't end there. I met an interesting man named Arni at the airport before flying back to the Philippines. He is a Filipino working as a US Navy for 20 years in San Diego, California. What surprised me was the fact that he was in my hometown Bohol, Philippines when it was hit by a 7.2 magnitude earthquake and he was there when Leyte was devastated by the super typhoon Yolanda. He was an amazing man; he survived for 2 days with nothing but a bottle of water. When I asked him if he was scared when he was in the midst of those calamities, he simply told me that he had four near-death experiences working as US Navy so he was used to the fact that his life was always at risk. I had a brief encounter with this man but he left a very important lesson. He reminded me to live my life to the fullest while I am still young; to always look at the brighter side of life despite the challenges and not to hold onto past regrets.

I had lots of good memories to treasure but the best thing I received was the friendships I gained, both from Indonesia and the

Philippines. I met a lot of different people which made my journey fun, exciting, and awesome beyond words! My experience was indeed a beautiful chapter in the book of my life and so I decided to add more beautiful chapters!

Realizing that life here on earth is a glimpse of heaven, I decided to bring heaven to others too.

It was a perfect Saturday night. I wanted to relive the good memories I had in Indonesia so I decided to munch on green tea ice cream. Remember in Indonesia I fell in love with it right away.

Michelle, my spiritual sister, was seated next to me and that made the night even more wonderful. We decided to stay for a couple of hours at Family Mart to satisfy my cravings. We talked about the amazing experience we had at Anawim, a home for abandoned elderly founded by Bo Sanchez, a Catholic lay preacher and author.

We were so immersed in our conversation that we didn't notice it was 3AM already. Then suddenly, a man sat beside me. He didn't say a word. After a few more minutes, he finally got the courage to join our conversation.

I looked at Michelle and she caught my gaze. We knew he sat there for a purpose and our instincts were right. He invited us to join his networking business.

As soon as he was done speaking, I asked him: "Why are you doing business?"

He gave me a puzzled look and then he answered: "To earn money of course!"

I asked again: "Aside from money, what else?"

He looked uncomfortable but still answered: "To help my family."

I asked again: "What else?"

He sighed and looked at me saying: "Why do you ask questions like that? Why are you not satisfied with my answers?"

I just smiled. Michelle and I explained to him how important it is to put God first in everything and encouraged him to offer his all to Him, including his business.

There was a moment of silence after that. Then I saw a tear drop fall from his eyes as he uttered: "Sorry God, I don't spend time with you anymore; I am too busy with many other things that you're not my priority anymore."

My heart was deeply moved and so was Michelle. So she started to ask him lots of questions to get to know more about him. He mentioned that his networking business is his part-time job so we asked what his full time job is.

He was silent for awhile and with his eyes fixed on the floor, he answered: "I am just a janitor."

I told him to stop looking down at the floor and to lift his gaze on me instead. I asked him: "Why do you seem so ashamed? You have a decent job! You must be proud!"

Giving me a surprised look he said: "Ma'am, you're the only one who appreciates me for having this job. I'm used to being laughed at when I tell people my job."

"Would you believe that she used to work as a house help before?" Michelle said pointing at me.

He looked at me with disbelief.

I nodded: "Yes, and I'm proud of it. I'll never be who I am now if not because of that. Continue to work hard so that you can reach your dreams in life with God."

He was teary-eyed again. He expressed his heartfelt thanks for the kind words he received from us. To our astonishment, he said: "Both of you speak with so much wisdom, why is that so?"

We answered: "Thanks to the Feast!"

Curiosity was written all over his face. Michelle asked him for a piece of paper, he took out his journal so Michelle wrote the address of The Feast Ortigas and also our mobile numbers.

He smiled as he said: "I hope we can be really good friends. I would love to hang out with people like you. Instead of you saying yes to my business proposal, I'm the one who's saying yes to your invitation to join The Feast."

We laughed at the turn of events, realizing how wonderful God's works are! Then I remembered we didn't get his name, so I asked: "We've been talking for hours now, what's your name by the way?"

He answered: "Jesus." And then he disappeared. (Haha! Just kidding! Of course he didn't vanish into thin air.)

Michelle and I exclaimed: "Seriously?"

Then he showed us his ID and we confirmed that his name was really Jesus. The following Monday after our encounter, we worshiped God with our new friend Jesus at The Feast Ortigas which brought us so much joy.

As I was reflecting on that incident, I realized that everyone needs Jesus.

I too, had an encounter with Jesus countless times and I'll share one instance that lingered in my heart up to now...

"One, two, three! Okay dear, one last step." Said Li, as she assisted her daughter Leraine to climb the stairs to their apartment.

I held back my tears as I looked at them.

Leraine's story is... At 12 years of age she had just won the quiz bee and table tennis for her school in 2004. But when she had a slight fever Li took her to the doctor. They could not find anything was wrong. Within 24 hours she was in a coma which lasted for 7 months. Then for 5 years she was completely bedridden, during which for 7 months she had to have tube feeding through her stomach. She was diagnosed with Japanese encephalitis. She can't see, her arms look deformed and her face looked like she just suffered from stroke. However, to me, Leraine has the most beautiful smile I have ever seen. The beauty of her soul radiates her whole being. She's so sweet and innocent.

Li and Leraine were introduced to me by Brendan. He met them at an adoration chapel where he felt called to approach them and prayed for Leraine outside the chapel afterwards. We were attending Brendan's presentation organized by Legion of Mary and Li was so kind to invite us to their house for dinner when it was over.

When I looked at Li her eyes spoke of audacity. That was the first time I met her, but for some reason I couldn't fathom, I felt in my heart that she'd been through a lot in life. Li started to share bits and pieces of her life. She shared how her husband left her when Leraine was still a baby. Li decided to do things on her own and she did her best to provide for Leraine's needs.

Everything seemed perfect at first, Leraine was an intelligent child until she got sick. Li had to stop working as an accountant to take care of her. At 22, Leraine could no longer do things on her own. Her life depended on her mother.

Curious as to how Li sustained their daily needs considering the cost of Leraine's medications, I asked her how she managed the finances knowing she quit her job. With a huge smile on Li's face, she answered: "God is the greatest provider." I smiled back at her, amazed with her deep faith.

Li left the apartment to buy dinner so I automatically assumed the mother role to Leraine. I approached her and she hugged me tightly. She showered me with kisses. So I returned her embrace with equal intensity. We hugged for what felt like an eternity when she uttered words that made me cry. She can hardly talk because of her illness, but despite that, she managed to say: "I love you" in stuttered speech.

My heart melted. It took her a few minutes to say those 3 words and I felt how hard she tried to make sure I understood what she said. I replied to her: "I love you too, God loves you and Mama Mary loves you". She nodded upon hearing my words and she kissed me on my cheek. The river of tears I was holding back when I first saw them flooded. I felt God's love in her embrace.

How about you? Do you feel God's love through the people He sends in your life? Or through His beautiful plans unfolding right before your very eyes?

Look around you. Do you realize that a beautiful flower was once a tiny bud? That the colorful butterfly smelling a flower's sweetness was once a defenseless caterpillar?

Now, look at yourself. You were once just a delicate being inside your mother's womb. Yet God who is so loving and generous brought you out to this world so you could see a glimpse of heaven and bring that heaven to others.

Prayer:

"Father God, thank you for letting me experience your love through the people in my life. Help me become like you to help others too. May I bring your love to everyone I meet. Help me appreciate all the blessings around me. Open my eyes to see the beauty of this world. Help me bring heaven here on earth. Amen."

God's Touch
© Brendan Roberts

The beauty of nature
Astounds, en-captures and enthralls.

From the grandeur of mountains,
To the calmness and power of the sea.
From the wonder of new life,
To the uniqueness of creation.

The Virgin forests,
Swarm with wildlife.
Beauty is in every living creature.

The raw power of the storm,
And the stillness of the lake,
Are enthralling in themselves.

All creation has one mark;
There is one print left on all Creation,
That is God's touch.

Chapter 14

GOD CHASES YOU

"There is no fear in love. But perfect love casts out fear, because fear has to do with punishment. The one who fears is not made perfect in love. We love because He first loved us (1 John 4:18-19)"

Do you know that God pursues you and will never stop doing so?

Because of His very nature, which is love, He longs to have a relationship with you. He created you for His glory.

God gives you love so that you will not be afraid. He wants to have a loving relationship with you.

Jesus willingly gives His life on the Cross for you. He is forever drawing you in fellowship with Him. A good relationship must be pursued and He pursues you with His perfect love.

Weng Masbate, my co-servant of The Feast Ortigas media ministry shared to me how God pursued her until she finally welcomed a life with Him:

I have grown up with a lot of resentment towards God. I go to Mass and pray because I don't want to be punished. I have to be good so that nothing bad is going to come to me.

When my father died, my father's family started to press on their rights for the family business. I was made to choose between what is right and what is good. I chose to protect my mom and my brothers; and I had to break that small bond that holds our family together with hurtful words. Also at that time my aunt whom I trusted, respected and loved so much turned away from me.

I never felt more alone and angrier than before. I had to ask if making a stand for my family was so wrong that God had to take away the only person I loved and trusted. I don't want a God who is like that. So from then I decided He would cease to exist in my life. I would forge through life on my own. I didn't need anyone and I definitely didn't need God! That's when all the invitations from religious organizations started to pour in. I insulted and yelled at anyone who tried to talk to me about a Father in heaven who loves me more than I can ever know. After that they stopped coming and I thought...peace at last.

Life was OK; I was achieving my goals and I received respect and admiration from friends and family. But I still felt empty that I found myself chasing after happiness on a day-to-day basis. I thought going out with "friends" was the answer, so I hung out with the party people and I spent time going to clubs, smoking and drinking. I didn't like it but I thought it was the only way to be accepted and I could be part of something. I never really thought that it was possible to be alone in a crowd.

I wanted to give up and end life altogether but I had a family to support. I didn't know who to talk to and didn't want to talk about it because I didn't want to appear weak in the eyes of other people. Before I went to sleep, I would relive all the painful experiences and upon waking up, I would start by cursing the day. With all the hurt bottled up within me, I became a very difficult person; I was hard on everyone around me including myself. I honestly didn't know why some people stuck by me because at these moments I had a capacity to turn people into saints with their patience and enduring love for me.

I reached the lowest point of my life in January 1996. I woke up in the middle of the night crying and immediately knelt down and prayed, "God, if you are real, take care of my family and you can use my hands to serve you."

After a series of events, I met a high school friend whom I didn't really like and she invited me to check out her business. She successfully invited me to a Life in the Spirit seminar by telling me that there would be a Mass plus a talk on how to be wealthy through God (it was a talk about tithing). Curiosity gripped me, so, even if I had no sleep yet, I went. Who doesn't want to be wealthy? I arrived almost at the end of the talk and was still amazed about the testimonies I was listening to about how God provides, loves and protects. "Who is that God?" I pondered. It was followed by a Healing Mass. I never cried as much as I did that day. On that day, God showed a vision of a covered well and when the cover was removed, all possibilities of my life with God came out. I cannot explain how I felt that day.

I attended prayer meetings every week. I experienced joy, healing and love from a God I never knew. I started experiencing my own miracles, and I was on fire with God's love. It was enough; finally, I found the love I was looking for.

God was faithful in taking care of my family. After two years, they can already stand on their own without my assistance. Freedom at last or so I thought. God started to ask me for my end of the commitment which I conveniently forgot. I was enjoying my new-found freedom. I said "NO, I am not ready!" God is a patient God and He knows that I am still new in the faith. So He gave me a few months before giving me the gift of spiritual dryness. I did not understand what was going on. I asked the elders what was the emptiness in my heart and I was told to look for God outside. I did not get it but I tried working on increasing my knowledge about God, so I started reading and attending Feast. I was also leading prayer meetings and handling the community activities in less than a year.

From time to time, God would ask me: "Are you ready?" I was scared because God always pushes me outside of my comfort zone so I said "NO!" I was longing for that "feeling-of-joy" in my heart and I couldn't find it. I asked God and He was silent. My elders gave me encrypted messages like, "God already wanted to marry you and you're not saying yes." I thought: "Am I supposed to become a nun?" So, I waited for the call.

While waiting I continued to grow in all other areas of my life. I became a totally different person: more confident, less angry, less afraid and I discovered a lot of new gifts that I never thought were there. I also quit smoking, drinking and partying because I changed my friends. It was an amazing journey of self-discovery but I was not satisfied with my relationship with God. It was an on and off again relationship. We had our arguments, yes I shouted at Him if I wanted to. I even told Him that it was His fault that I was so stubborn because He made me. That's how confident I was that God loves me.

Then, in 2013 another turning point happened. I experienced failure after failure: in my business, in my job, in my health, in my relationships with the people around me and in my service, everything was crumbling. I was so busy that I couldn't even stop to pray or tell myself to slow down. I spiraled down the road of depression. I knew that I needed help and I had no one to turn to because everyone was also busy. So, I dropped everything.

God tried to talk to me in several ways and I ignored those attempts until I took my pen and notebook again. I started writing, pouring out my angst, my disappointments and anger towards God. He listened when I needed someone to listen. He talked when I needed advice. He didn't give up on me when I already gave up on myself. He was not a push-over because even on the many nays I said He kept on asking until I finally said "Yes!" Then, I attended Love Life retreat. It was then that everything went full circle. I finally understood what God was trying to communicate to me.

In my journey, it was God who picked me up when I was so broken; I thought I was beyond repair and He called me His. He believed in me and pushed me to my limits that made me realize how strong and wonderfully made I am. I saw my own beauty when I started to see myself through His eyes. I started to love myself and the people around me because I am loved by my Father in heaven. He made me realize that I am worth all the effort and the entire waiting. I also understood He was not calling me to become a nun. I realized I was so attached to the feeling of joy in my heart, just like the feeling of being in love. He made me see that real love starts when falling in love ends.

I also learned that I love the right one if I am becoming a better person and I am like that with God first. I don't know where this journey will lead me and I am choosing to take it one day at a time. As long as I am holding God's hand, I know I will be happy. *The End*

Being alone with Jesus, a genuine one-to-one personal relationship with the Lord, is the greatest relationship you can have for a lifetime.

One of my closest friends shared to me how her life had changed when she realized God had been pursuing her. She had been through so much that at one point she hated life. She was molested by her own father. I love how she shared her story of finding love in God and looking up to Him as the eternal Father as her earthly father failed her:

"He never let go of my hand. During those darkest moments when I wanted to leave Him, He led my feet even closer to Him. When I wanted to succumb to sin, when I planned to waste my life by taking drugs and any other vices like smoking and drinking, He gave me the grace to respect my body, the temple of His Holy Spirit. Being molested by my own father, I wanted to give in to sexual immorality but God revealed to me that my purity is a gift from Him."

Even if you fall short of God's glory, He is still there waiting for you to reignite your relationship with Him.

God is the sun that never sets. He always makes His light available for you 24/7. Set a special time for God and date Him every day. He must be the last thought before you sleep and the first thought when you wake up.

Prayer:

"Loving Father, thank you for tirelessly pursuing me until I found myself in your arms again. Thank you for loving me even during those times that I could not even love myself. Thank you for not giving up on me, for patiently waiting for me. Help me to build a loving relationship with you. Grant me the perseverance to seek you and make you my number one priority. In Jesus mighty name, Amen."

My Father's Eyes
© Brendan Roberts

You long to believe,
But you can't.
Something is holding you back;

Deep down you are afraid.
You are afraid that is a big joke;
That it is all a big deception.

But the biggest gamble is ahead;
The gamble which could cost your soul.

You see Christians who are hypocrites,
But also Christians who genuinely love.
The answer I have for you my friend,
Is to look into my Father's eyes.

You will find tremendous love,
A love that will sweep through you;
Touching the depths of your soul.

The love will challenge and heal you;
Look deeper and the love
Will remove your confusion and doubts.

Do not be afraid my friend;
Look into God the Father's eyes.

Chapter 15

FINDING LOVE GOD'S WAY

"Who shall separate us from the love of Christ? Shall trouble or hardships or persecution or famine or nakedness or danger or sword? No, in all these things we are more than conquerors through Him who loved us. For I am convinced that neither death nor life, neither angels nor demons, neither the present nor the future, nor any powers, neither height nor depth, nor anything else in all creation, will be able to separate us from the love of God that is in Christ Jesus our Lord." – Romans 8:35-39

I was in prison of a desire for appreciation of my own self-worth, until I found my freedom in God. The desire to be recognized grew in my heart for I wanted to prove my worth.

I did things that didn't make me happy at all; I was struggling to be the kind of person other people wanted me to be until it dawned on me that I could be my real unique self.

At one point in my life, during the darkest hours of my days, I told my friend: "I'm tired. I just want to escape from life's misery. The idea of going to a place where no one knows me was so tempting.

My friend answered: "So you want to rest!"

The tone of her voice seemed like she was ready to kill me. So in no time I explained: "Not really rest in peace forever in a tomb, but I just want to find myself."

The words that came out of her mouth pierced me like a double-edged sword: "To know thyself, know thy God."

In hopes of finding my lost self, I decided to re-read the Bible like it was my first time. I chose to fall in love with God again by the words He spoke in the Bible. True enough, I found my identity in Him and His message was clear: to make Him known in my life.

Manilyn Fernandez, my friend and co-servant of Feast Ortigas pastoral ministry shared her story of searching for love and finding it in God:

Growing up in a poor and big family, living in a province and studying in a public school were the painful realities which resulted in my insecurities in life.

I couldn't even look people straight in the eyes, I felt ugly. I lived my life pleasing other people.

Beautiful women to me were pain in the eyes. I'd always scrutinized them to find their flaws and imperfections. I mocked them in my head.

I would praise successful people around me but deep inside, I envied and despised them. I didn't even mingle with rich people because I was afraid they would reject me just because I didn't know how to speak English. I was aware I should not feel that way but I didn't know how to get rid of my bitterness towards other people who I thought were better than me.

My insecurities grew when my then boyfriend dumped me for another woman. That was when I hit rock bottom in life. I cried myself to sleep every night and I thought my life had no meaning at all. I lost sight of the beauty of the world.

I was consumed by my past mistakes, rejections, trials, shameful experiences and failures. I welcomed the bad thoughts and all the negative feelings from the enemy. I suffered depression.

After two months of soaking myself in deep sorrow, I decided to talk to God. I had no other choice; I blamed Him for everything that had happened in my life.

I threw hurtful words at God then suddenly, I felt sorry for everything I'd said and done. I asked for His forgiveness and surrendered to Him. I didn't hear Him answer. However talking to Him somehow massaged my calloused heart.

I couldn't thank God enough for keeping me away from the evil things people suffering from depression resort to. Despite the terrible pain, I didn't turn to drugs or alcohol. I knew it was through God's divine intervention.

I found myself searching for God and I allowed Him to reveal His purpose for me. He did not fail me.

When I decided to nurse my wounded heart He brought me to a spiritual community, *The Feast Ortigas*.

I desired to get to know God more and slowly I understood why I had to go through painful situations.

Every talk series of my spiritual community pierced my heart. I felt God was the one speaking to me, healing me, enlightening me.

Slowly, I got back the zest for life I had once lost. I gained wisdom from God and I started knowing myself in a deeper sense. Belonging to a spiritual community was very powerful in times of depression.

In my search to fully grasp why I felt so insecure about myself, I looked back on everything that had happened in the past and pondered it in my heart.

I then realized that my love tank (heart) was empty. I started reading spiritual books which I never did before. Then I was enlightened to examine myself deeply; I found out that my love tank was empty because I didn't feel loved by my family. I tried to fill the emptiness in my heart through my relationship with my ex-boyfriend to the point that even if I knew I was in a wrong relationship, I kept on clinging onto him rather than to God. I thought the attention I was getting from the man I loved would fill the longings of my heart.

I stopped seeking love from people and started searching for the most powerful love only God could give.

Answers came when I allowed my heart to be captured by God. I found pure joy resulting from an intimate relationship with Him.

I finally decided to change the way I saw myself. As my eyes were fixed on God, I learned to affirm and love myself the way God loved me. I finally accepted my own uniqueness.

I realized that all of my problems and struggles were caused by the lack of love for myself and my relationship with God.

Now, I'm not saying that I'm living in a bed of roses; I still go through trials in life but instead of complaining to God, I just say to myself that behind this is a treasure waiting to be discovered, an opportunity for me to grow by leaps and bounds. Instead of figuring out everything I will just have faith in His words from Romans 8:28: "Everything will work out for your own good to those who love God and are called according to his purpose".

I laughed remembering the times I begged God to bring my boyfriend back but here I was kneeling, thanking Him and worshiping Him for saving me from the wrong guy.

Those moments that I felt so small and worthless, I couldn't imagine how my life would be if I continued to let the enemy manipulate my thinking and deceive me into believing all those lies.

As I started to love myself and lived in Godfidence (God's confidence), I felt happiness and contentment that I had never experienced before.

Truly, when you experience God personally, your life will never be the same again. Your life will find its meaning and purpose and He will affirm you that you are fearfully and wonderfully made because He made you in His own image and likeness. Holding onto this truth, I'm confident that God will bring out the best version of myself; the woman He always wanted me to be.

In finding God, I found not only myself, I found the greatest love I can call my own.

Prayer:

"Father God, thank you for the love I can call my own. Thank you for helping me emerge victorious amidst the trials in my life. Truly, you are the source of true love; the only one who can satisfy the deepest longings of my heart."

Be Satisfied With Me
By Saint Anthony of Padua

Everyone longs to give themselves completely to someone,
to have a deep soul relationship with another,
to be loved thoroughly and exclusively.
But God says: "No, not until you are satisfied,
fulfilled and content by being loved by Me alone.
With giving yourself totally and unreservedly to Me,
with having an intensely personal and unique relationship with Me alone.
Discovering that only in Me is your satisfaction to be found.
Will you be capable of the perfect human relationship that I have planned for you?
You will never be completely united with another
until you are united with Me;
exclusive of anyone or anything else
exclusive of any other desires or longings.

I want you to stop planning, to stop wishing and allow Me to
give you the most thrilling plan existing,
one you cannot imagine.
I want you to have the best,
Please allow Me to bring it to you...
So just keep watching Me,
expecting the greatest things,
Keep experiencing the satisfaction that I am,
Keep listening and learning the things that I tell you.
Just wait...
That's all.
Don't be anxious.
Don't worry.
Don't look at the things others have received
or that I have given them.
Don't look around at the things you think you want.
Just keep looking off and away up to Me
or you'll miss what I want to show you.
And then, when you're ready,
I'll surprise you with a love
far more wonderful than you could dream of...
You see, until you are ready,
and until the one I have for you is ready,
I am working even at this moment
to have both of you ready at the same time.
Until you are both satisfied exclusively with Me
and the life I prepared for you,
you won't be able to experience the love that exemplifies
your relationship with Me, and this is the perfect love...
And dear one, I want you to have the most wonderful love,
I want you to see in the flesh a picture of your relationship
with Me and to enjoy materially and concretely the everlasting
union of beauty, perfection, and love that I offer you with
Myself.
Know that I love you utterly.
I am God. Believe it and be satisfied.

Chapter 16

CONCLUSION

"When will you be in a relationship?" This question has always been thrown at me.

My answer always has been: "I'm already in a relationship. I have the greatest boyfriend a woman could ever have!"

Next question my friends would ask: "Who is he?"

Flashing a big smile on my face, I answered: "J.C."

"Who is J.C?"

"He's the man who died on the Cross, who unselfishly shed His blood in the name of love."

Wait, don't fret nor panic. I didn't write this book with the goal of making you an old maid. Some have the special calling for single blessedness or the religious life as well as marriage. I want you to be at peace with your singleness and vocation. Discern your calling. Chances are you'll spend more years in marriage than being single. If you are called to the vocation of marriage, believe in your heart that God will not make you single a day longer than He planned. Trust that He has written a love story far more beautiful than the ones you saw in the movies or you've read from romance novels.

Have you given your sweetest "yes" to God? Before you should give your "yes" to a man whether it is in response to "Will you be my girlfriend?" or "Will you marry me?" you should give your wholehearted "Yes!" to God first.

Jesus is a determined lover who will never give up on you no matter what. If your suitor promises to bring down the moon and the stars at your feet to win your heart, God promises you more than anything else in this world: HIMSELF.

Seeking Jesus is the greatest adventure, finding Him is the greatest achievement and falling in love with Him is the greatest romance.

There will always be an emptiness in your heart that only God can fill. Jesus not only wants you to get to heaven, He wants you to experience heaven here on earth for you to bring heaven to others as well.

Salvation is a gift from God. What you need to do is accept Him as your personal Lord and Savior and obey all of His commands including within a Church community. Once you open your heart to His love, it will be impossible for you not to love Him back. The wisest moment in your life happens when you say "Yes!" to God.

I once read a Facebook post of a friend: "Stop waiting for your Mr Right. Get up and find him. He must be stuck on a tree or something." I laughed but somehow, I panicked.

The pressure of knowing that almost all of my high school and college batch-mates were already getting married, being invited to christening events, engagement parties, marriage proposals, bridal showers and wedding feasts, I decided to find love my way and not God's way.

There was this guy who had been too close to my heart that it came to a point when what I thought was just a God-centered friendship developed into wishing him to be the man whom I would be with for the rest of my life. We went out occasionally; shared each other's blessings and trials, ate and prayed together. We talked about everything under the sun for long hours either on the phone or when our schedules met. I could still remember how I used to put my hands on my chest to feel the fast beating of my heart each time he would drop me home. (As soon as I closed the door behind him of course! Haha). Everything seemed too perfect; as if a love story was about to blossom. Until I realized that I was soaked in an undefined relationship which had taken my time off from God.

In my hopes to find Mr Right above God's timing, I pulled myself down to the pit of throbbing pain. Thanks to God's grace, I had the courage to block him from my life. Don't get me wrong though, I'm grateful for whatever we had in the past, in fairness to him, he made me feel special. My prayer has now been transformed as I aligned my wishes to God's purposes. Before, I prayed that he would be the right man for me. Now, I pray that he would strive to be a man after God's own heart to that woman God has prepared for him. I used to pray that I would be the right woman for him. Now, I pray that I will be Miss Right to that someone God has prepared for me. I thank God for allowing me to experience that particular chapter in my life; it was painful, but I learned a lot from it.

You see, the first move isn't finding Mr Right but striving to become Miss Right through God's grace. Instead of praying for God to deliver your prince charming straight to your doorstep, strive on becoming the woman that suits the prayer of a man who longs for a woman of substance and character.

Don't get too focused on imagining how great you would look wearing your wedding gown, or in listing the names of people who would complete your wedding entourage. (With the name of groom left as blank! Haha.) The wedding ceremony will only last for a few hours but marriage lasts for a lifetime. Above anything else, prepare your heart.

Marriage is a walk down a path of roses with thorns. Don't expect that everything will be as smooth-sailing as the first day when you both fell in love with each other. You need to examine yourself the same way you scrutinize how you look in front of the mirror before you go out on your first date. Just as how keen you are in observing the pimples on your face. Notice how you've grown as a woman of wisdom.

The following are the crucial questions you need to ask yourself before your most awaited "I DO" moment:

* "Do I have a personal relationship with God?"

Only when your heart is overflowing with love from God can you share pure love to others. Remember that someday, you will be the light of your own home. But how can you do that if you're in darkness? As what the Bible says in Luke 6:39 "Can the blind lead the blind? Will they not both fall into a pit?" Come to the ultimate source of light. Be a woman after God's own heart by reading His word every day. Go out on a date with God. Just be with Him, soak yourself in His presence. You can have your "alone time" with Him in your room, inside the adoration chapel, or at a park where your eyes will be filled with His wonderful creation.

* "Do I love myself just the way I am?"

You cannot give what you don't have. Before you can love others freely, you need to love yourself first. Look at the mirror and tell yourself: "I love me for who I was, who I am, and who I will become". God loves you as you are, including your scars, wounds, curves and edges. He loves even the things that you hate about yourself. He accepts all your perceived physical imperfections. God loves you as you are and He loves you too much to leave you that way. Stop being hard on yourself. Stop wishing you were somebody else. You are beautiful just the way you are because you are God's princess, you are His daughter.

* "Have I learned the essence of being selfless, of dying to my own selfish desires to attend to the needs of others?"

When you get married, your purpose is to be the best mom and wife that you can be. You have to put aside your own wants and prioritize the needs of your kids. There would be times you will be tired from work yet you still have to serve your husband. You might have to give up that wonderful dress you've been eying for so long just so you can grant your child's Christmas wish. This is just a simple example. Being a mom and wife takes a lot of sacrifices in the name of love. While you're still single, practice being selfless by serving others starting with your parents down to everyone around you. Remember that what you do for others, you do it to God also.

* "Have I learned the basics of financial management?"

Have you heard the popular cliché "When poverty walks through the door, love flies out the window"? It's the commitment that sustains love, not the feeling. And part of that commitment is the financial aspect of the relationship. You should know how to use your money wisely. For married couples, it is often the wife who budgets the money. Right now, learn to distinguish between wants and needs. 10-20-70 method works. As soon as you receive your salary, set aside 10 % for the Lord, 20% for savings, and 70% for your expenses. Being able to afford something doesn't mean you should buy it. Save and invest for a good return.

* "Am I living a pure, chaste life?"

Save yourself wholeheartedly for your future husband — physically, spiritually and emotionally. If you have surrendered "your all" to your ex-boyfriend or your current boyfriend, ask

God for a second chance of purity and believe in your heart that it will be given to you through God's grace. If you are Catholic, go to the Sacrament of Reconciliation and experience God's healing love.

Overwhelmed at the many things that you need to do before you can be Miss Right? The Bible says it best:

> When one finds a worthy wife, her value is far beyond pearls. Her husband, entrusting his heart to her, has an unfailing prize. She brings him good, and not evil, all the days of her life. She obtains wool and flax and works with loving hands. She puts her hands to the distaff, and her fingers ply the spindle. She reaches out her hands to the poor, and extends her arms to the needy. Charm is deceptive and beauty fleeting; the woman who fears the Lord is to be praised. Give her a reward of her labors, and let her works praise her at the city gates (Proverbs 31:10-13, 19-20, 30-31).

Becoming Miss Right cannot be achieved overnight. It's a continuous process, a decision you have to make each day. It is a commitment to the Lord that you will strive to be the woman He intended you to be. Each time you stumble, get up! Stand firm and remember not to give up because your Mr Right is just around the corner. Don't worry, God is holding his hands just as He holds yours too so that one day, when both of you are ready, you will hold hands together, with God at the center. :)

WORTH CHASING

PURSUING LOVE
GOD'S WAY

BRENDAN ROBERTS

*Kiwi Graphix Publishing
New Zealand*

Copyright © 2015 Brendan Roberts and Erlita Suarez Cabal

All rights reserved

Published by Kiwi Graphix

ISBN 978-0-473-31939-7 (Same ISBN as Worth the Chase)

Cover design © Michelle Dineros

Unless otherwise noted Scripture is quoted from the New Revised Standard Version Bible.

Printed 2015

Contents

Introduction	112
Chapter 1: Love Letter from God the Father	114
Chapter 2: Do you Love Your Creative Self?	116
Chapter 3: Easy Woman or Woman of Faith?	119
Chapter 4: Discussing those Taboo Subjects	121
Chapter 5: Shattered Heart to Embracing Christ	126
Chapter 6: Spiritual Athleticism	131
Chapter 7: Listen Lord, Your Servant is Speaking	137
Chapter 8: Do Real Men Go to Church?	142
Chapter 9: The Poor Captured my Heart	147
Chapter 10: God's Living Image	152
Chapter 11: Transformation to Greatness	156
Chapter 12: Drinking for Pleasure or to Oblivion	160
Chapter 13: Why Surrender Your All?	163
Chapter 14: The Thrill of the Chase	170
Chapter 15: Fear Not for God Equips and Sends You	174
Chapter 16: Conclusion	177
Author's Note	180
Ohter Books by Brendan Roberrs	182
Facebook Groups	184
Last Message from the Authors	185

Dedication

Firstly I dedicate this book to Monsignor Vincent Hunt who passed on to heaven before I started writing this book. You have been such a fantastic mentor, friend and help in my writing. Thank you from the bottom of my heart!

Once again, I would also like to dedicate this book to all those who have supported me in my writing. It is ever more my mission and it touches my heart that you have believed in me through the hardest times. I'm so grateful for the support that I've had from strangers and friends alike. With each book someone else is brought into my life to give priceless assistance, and this in itself is quite remarkable and I must thank God for that.

To Elly, my co-author who was inspired with the titles of both books and who became my best friend in such a short time. Thank you for asking me to mentor you. As a result I showed myself how to focus on writing and was able to complete this book in just six weeks together with "Our Father Where Art My Pay: A Call to Holiness in the Workplace". I am so proud of you; that you endured through the toughest times. God is truly the author of both of these books.

Most importantly, I dedicate this book primarily to God Our Father, Jesus Christ our redeemer and the Holy Spirit who makes us more like Christ.

ADGM

Introduction

I am writing this book while on a personal mission to the Philippines. The experiences in this country will stay with me for a long time, maybe even for the rest of my life. Visiting a poverty-stricken country really opens up one's eyes and even heart to those who are less fortunate than us. With a third of the Filipino's under the poverty line it seems like a daunting task and some may even revert to Christ's words, "The poor you will always have with you (Matthew 26:11)."

I truly marvel at how God brought me into the life of the author of this book. After meeting Elly she asked me to be her mentor. Little did I know that God wanted us to mentor each other. This has developed into a wonderful friendship. In fact she is now a best friend.

Being in the Philippines I was surrounded by many beautiful women. It can truly make a man's head spin. But God brought me back down to earth. As His disciple, His son, I was called to have purity of heart and not to flirt with the ladies.

As a man it is tempting to flirt with women. It is easy to take notice of the beautiful women one comes across. Therefore one takes a second lingering look at the gorgeous woman in the street, or waiting at the elevator. Then it is easy for the mind to wander and even the imagination to run wild.

Even if it is just a lingering look without the mind playing gymnastics it is not healthy. God's way is to see every woman as beautiful. Even more importantly the soul of the woman must be beautiful and then radiate and emphasize her outer beauty. Who really wants a model who is cold as ice? Or a model who has no compassion for those God is calling you to have compassion for, the poor.

This book was the brainchild of my now best friend, Elly. But even more importantly it was truly inspired by the Holy Spirit.

When God wrote her a love letter which He wanted her to bless women with, she shared it with me. I was so inspired by

Introduction

that letter. Men you should really read it! It is truly amazing! God really spoke to her powerfully. I absolutely loved it and being a man I had some comments to make, including some witty ones. So Elly said I should write one inspired by God for men.

So picture this. One evening after attending Mass and adoration my phone is charging at the wall and I'm standing next to it. I have one thought which sparks the "Love Letter from God the Father". I'm typing into my phone notes with one finger and the letter just flows.

I was amazed with what God was saying. So I shared it with Elly after we went for a run, read the Mass readings of the day and shared how it related to our lives. I also prayed for God's inspiration for her writing that day. When I shared God's letter she was deeply touched by it and then she felt that this book which she was writing for women should be a combination — one half written to women and the other half to men. So she asked me to write the other half. Wow!

Then I went to the nearby adoration chapel. I said to God He could say anything He liked. God surely wanted to speak. I didn't know, but His love letter wasn't finished. So the second period of inspiration for that love letter happened right there in the chapel. I was armed with pen and my prayer diary. It was there that the words just flowed again. So please read on to see what God wants to say to men. Before you continue reading ask God to open your heart to what He wants to reveal through this book for you and anyone else who reads it. May the words touch your heart and inspire you to seek Him more than anything.

Chapter 1

LOVE LETTER FROM GOD THE FATHER

Dear son, the ladies are crying because they feel too short, too fat or even too skinny. A small pimple on the face seems to them like a mountain. As for you, you think you're not successful enough, don't have big enough muscles or abs, not talented or not as good looking as Tom Cruise or Arnold Schwarznegger.

Joking aside I created you and when you seek me with all your heart I am so proud of you. Does your chasing after so many women fulfill you? Only I can truly fulfill you.

Run to me, I'm waiting for you. Don't feed your ego. Feed your soul with my living word and my Body, the living Bread. I not only want to sustain, nourish and purify your soul, I want you to be transformed into a living image of me.

No matter what you have done in the past, I love you. I'm waiting for you to come into my presence, to fall to your knees before the Blessed Sacrament and to receive the bountiful graces I want to lavish upon you.

My son, practice the art of listening. Firstly come to me in prayer, especially before the Blessed Sacrament and listen to me. And listen to me through my word.

When you listen with your heart you will be even more of a blessing to those in your life. Listen first and then speak.

Seek me with your whole heart and you will be surprised. You will not be disappointed. Trust in my wonderful plan for you. Give me your dreams, your heart's desires, your regrets, your pain, your fears. I want to transform them so that you can image me and be who you are called to be. It is only through surrendering these, all of you, that you will be fully alive. I want to give you joy that the world cannot give. My joy lasts, even amidst your greatest struggles.

I love you my son. I died for you. I have loved you for all eternity and my love for you will never become any less. Like a fire my love blazes for you. All you have to do is follow me, obey all my commandments, including eating my Body and drinking my Blood and I will raise you up on the last day. Also love me with all you are and use that love to love others. Remember that I have all the graces that you need for my yoke is easy and my burden is light.

I will always love you my son. I delight in you. I rejoice in you. Through the sacraments I live in you and you in me. We are so intimately united. That is how passionately I love you. I am waiting for you to run to me in the Sacrament of Reconciliation. I offer you endless graces to forgive you and to fortify your soul.

My son you do not have to strive to be best at all costs. I call for your faithfulness to me through my living word and my Church. I gave you both Scripture and Tradition which are one. They form one organic whole because they come from the same source, Me. So love both.

So you want to be a man? Then trust in me and treat my princesses with pure love. If you seek after me and have a pure heart you will see me. Your friendships will be wholesome and you will open yourself to endless possibilities. With a pure heart you allow me to give you the right princess. Do not strive for love, but love me first. I seek your love most of all. Only then can you truly love anyone, friend or your heart's desire.

Love is a gift. You must submit yourself to my will and say, "Not my will but Yours be done, Lord". For some I call to single blessedness, never to marry; others to the consecrated religious life — just look at my beautiful nuns shining out my love and purity who dedicate their whole lives to me. Finally I call men to be my priests. They are consecrated, set apart for me and to serve me and the Church. These sons have great responsibility, love after my own heart, and I equip them for this great calling. Do not fear such a calling my son.

Others I call to express my love uniquely through the Sacrament of Marriage through which they must be open to my generous blessing, new life.

My son, submit to the calling I place on your life. Trust in my wonderful plan for you. Together we can change the world. Will you surrender everything, all you are, to me and allow me to transform you into a beautiful diamond as a gift for yourself and others? You were raw rock and you can be a priceless diamond. The choice is yours. Hold onto your life or give it completely to me.

Chapter 2

DO YOU LOVE YOUR CREATIVE SELF?

"As for you, you think you're not successful enough or even not talented or not as good looking as Tom Cruise or Arnold Schwarznegger."
From Love Letter from God

Image, image, image. Our culture and the influences of society form our image. All around us we have huge pressure to conform to the wider world. Here in the Philippines the billboards are enormous. Good looking men smile at you from the billboards, with perfect skin and perfect teeth care of Photoshop.

Often our parents will also influence our image. They will compliment us, call us handsome or they negatively influence our image. They may joke that we were actually adopted or have our father's genes or mother's genes if they don't like the way we look. Or they may compare us to our siblings. As a result we strive to win the affection of our parents and falling short of our siblings we feel bad.

Maybe like me, you were teased at school. So you developed a low self-esteem and hate the way you look. Sadly even rock stars have hated how they looked. They believed the lie that they had to look a certain way and even had to look perfect. For example, Michael Jackson had so many visits to the plastic surgeon. Sadly in the end he looked worse than when he started. But his self-image meant he did not love himself and so sought to change the way he looked.

You may feel that you lack any talent. But we are all talented or can develop a talent as we are created in the image and likeness of God. Because God is creative then you have the innate ability to be creative. Does that mean we will all be excellent basketball players? No way! We need to find our passion and develop our talents. All the famous stars, whether in sports or the movies had to work very hard to get to where they are now. The best will practice, practice and practice.

We should seek our image from our loving God, not from the wider world.

We may think that we are not successful enough. While it's important to seek success in one's life, we must be careful that we do not do so at the expense of our relationship with God. Many people put God aside when they are passionately driving for success. They think they have no time to pray as they seek that success.

We also need to ask ourselves what our motivation for such success is. Are we seeking success to feed our ego or are we seeking success so that we can provide for our future family? Are we seeking success so that we will have more money to spend on the ladies? Are we seeking success so that we can buy more luxury items so that we can show off to others?

God will not love you any more if you are successful. His love for you is unconditional. I've heard the saying that we should seek riches so then we can help others. But God is not asking us to wait until we have more money to help others. He is calling us to have generous hearts now. In fact Sacred Scripture is clear when it comes to helping those who beg. In the Gospel of Matthew Jesus says "Give to everyone who begs from you (Matthew 5:42)."

So what does God say about us? If we explore Sacred Scripture, the word of God we can discover much about what God says about us. Psalm 139 says that God formed you in your mother's womb (verse 13). A little later in that Psalm He says: "In your book were written all the days that were formed for me, when none of them as yet existed (verse 16)." That is why God has had you on his mind for all eternity. In other words God is saying, "I love you so much. I love you infinitely. Before time began I loved you. For all time I will love you."

He also displays His great love for you when He says: "I have carved you on the palm of my hands (Isaiah 49:16)." I have heard people say that they think God has forgotten them but God says "Can a woman forget her nursing child, or show no compassion for the child of her womb? Even these may forget, yet I will not forget you (Isaiah 49:151)."

God loves you with an everlasting love (see Jeremiah 31:3). You are a child of God because you received Him and believe in His name (see John 1:12). God chose you before the foundations of the world to be holy and blameless before Him in love (see

Ephesians 1:4). Because you follow Jesus you have the light of life (see John 8:12). Your body is the temple of the Holy Spirit, bought by the death and resurrection of Christ and you are not your own (see 1 Corinthians 6:19). You are Jesus' friend because He has revealed everything He heard from the Father (see John 15:15).You are an heir (inheritor) of God and joint heir with Christ provided that you share in His suffering so as to share in His glory (Romans 8:17). You can help complete what is lacking in Christ's afflictions for the sake of His body, the Church (see Colossians 1:24). You are a sheep of the Good shepherd who knows Jesus and He knows you (John 10:14). You are blessed with every spiritual blessing (Ephesians 1:3); have access to God in boldness and confidence through faith in Him (Ephesians 3:12); have life in you by eating the Flesh of the Son of Man and drinking His Blood (John 6:53-4) including eternal life now and Christ will raise you up on the last day as a result. You are called to be a saint who is faithful in Christ Jesus (Ephesians 1:1). God will supply your every need according to His riches in glory (Philippians 4:19).

So Sacred Scripture is very clear that God loves you passionately and eternally. I know it can feel awkward as a bloke (man) to think of loving God. But remember that God is love. He is the source of love. So we shouldn't be feeling uneasy about seeking to love Him with all that we are.

Chapter 3

EASY WOMAN OR WOMAN OF FAITH?

Guys let's be honest now. Do you really want an easy woman or a woman of faith, someone who will keep faithful to you in mind and heart? Do you really want to have a relationship with someone who has had sex with many men and has no problem with, even desiring sex on your first date or before marriage? I know in the west we would call this going to all the bases, rather than the first base of holding hands. But is it really a game? Do you think God desires us to see women as part of a game or to see them as having inherent dignity as children of God?

For any ladies reading this, that goes for you too. For those women who lead a man on and then step on his heart as if he is worthless do you think that is treating sons of God as having an inherent dignity given by God?

Let's look at the easy woman concept in another way. Guys, do you want to marry an easy woman who has had multiple sexual partners, who has in effect given part of her soul away to many men and will even subconsciously compare your intimacy with her past sexual experiences? I'm excluding here someone who deeply regrets living the easy lifestyle or giving up her virginity, repents and seeks God's forgiveness to change. This is what we call a spiritual virgin. It is clear that sexual intercourse is both spiritual and physical. Sacred Scripture even tells us this because the two become one flesh. How could they be so united if it was only physical?

Men your future spouse, or any women mind you, are not cars or trucks or even a jeepney where you can "try before you buy." Yes you can take out vehicles on a test run to see that what you buy will actually perform well. But sadly many think that they can have a test run in a relationship by seeing if they are compatible sexually and even test running their relationship as marriage by moving in together. Studies clearly show that these relationships are much more likely to end than a real marriage.

OK guys regarding the *try before you buy* concept your wallet may be empty from spending on gifts to impress your lady or paying for the multiple dates until she finally agrees to be your girlfriend, lol.

We must remember that women are not an object to be used or abused. So why entertain such a mentality of trying someone out sexually? If God has destined you to be together you will be compatible and so totally fine in that area. True love is not about how I am being pleased but how can I give of myself totally to my spouse, including pleasing my wife sexually.

Your future wife is not a racehorse, even if she nags you, lol. That's a pun (joke) because a slang term for a horse is a nag. She is not a racehorse where you can force her to do what you want or whip her emotionally. No matter what sex we are we should not give the other the cold shoulder which can be a form of manipulation to get what we want. Another way of emotionally whipping your partner is by being overly jealous or possessive. Such people reveal insecurities in themselves and that they don't trust the person they say they love. It is completely natural for women to have other men friends and chat with them through social media. Remember guys women are not to be treated as possessions that we own.

Are Church going women really more boring than easy women? There is often the misconception that women of faith are more boring. If you consider exciting doing things that are against God's ways then yes they will be boring. But if you consider doing God's will as He knows the best then we will lead such exciting and even adventurous lives.

God is calling us to a higher standard as men. We will cover this later in this book.

Chapter 4

DISCUSSING THOSE TABOO TOPICS

Guys there are topics that we are very reluctant or even afraid to ask our girlfriends. But as Catholic Christians there are one's that are vital to raise in discerning our future spouse.

IS ARTIFICIAL CONTRACEPTION AGAINST LIFE?

Firstly have you had the contraception conversation with your girlfriend? I'm definitely not going the way of the world and saying you should ask her if she uses condoms or even using the "safe sex" mantra myth. In fact the safest sex is no sex — keeping one's pants on.

So what am I referring to then? Just bare with me. If you are a man or woman after God's own heart then you won't use artificial contraception to block God's gift of life. OK, stop having a heart attack over this and hear me out. Don't burn this book or even throw it out the window. If you are a Christian and thus after God's own heart you will know that God gave us the Catholic Church, founded on the Apostles and that He promised His Holy Spirit to be with this support and pillar of truth (1 Timothy 3:15) until the end of time. If God wants to safeguard truth He will do so and does so through the areas of faith and morals.

So why is the Catholic Church so passionately against artificial contraception used to prevent pregnancy? Shouldn't one be able to have control over their own body? As already covered your body is not your own, it was purchased by Christ. Also when it comes to sexual intercourse it involves both body and soul and if new life eventuates then that gift of life is a responsibility. That new life must be safeguarded, cherished, protected and nurtured, not destroyed.

Let's look at the hierarchy of intentions when a married couple is considering planning to have what the Church calls the *supreme gift of God*, children, for example through Natural Family Planning with good intentions. The Church uses the term the *morally correct level of children*. In order to establish this level one needs to consider their own duties towards:

- God
- Themselves
- Towards their family and towards society.

But secular society turns this inside out, discarding God from the process and putting themselves in place of God. As I covered in my previous book, *Crusades Rediscovered* the couple "is called to consider their duties towards God first, then towards themselves (e.g. state of their health), the good of their family (their financial position, for example their bank is ready to foreclose on them) and the good of society, for example low population rate and low Church attendance."[1]

Therefore the Church supports the spacing out of children for good intentions.

When it comes to contraception there are other things that need to be considered. If your girlfriend wants to use contraception sadly she opens herself to the death of an embryo, which is a living person. She may not intentionally be open to the death of such a person but it is a known consequence of the pill and other abortifacients which result in the death of the unborn child. The pill stops the embryo (Latin of fetus: offspring) from implanting into the wall of the uterus.

Therefore it is imperative in discerning if one's girlfriend is the person to marry that one have these discussions on what they believe in relation to sex outside of the covenant of marriage, and artificial contraception used to block God's *supreme gift*.

Finally folks there is one more very difficult discussion that one needs to have; that difficult topic is one that men run from like running from a nagging woman or a woman who is angry, lol. This topic is one which is surrounded by lies, especially that it's only a woman's issue. That topic is, abortion. It is so important because unless she truly believes all that the Catholic Church *believes, professes* and *teaches to be revealed by God* or is simply pro-life from conception to natural death then you need to know or else your living image could be killed in the future. So it's vital to know if she would ever consider having an abortion herself. While this discussion is surrounded by emotions the mother should always protect her child even if she had to give up her own life. It is never right to intentionally kill a child, unborn or born.

Obviously this isn't a discussion to have on your first date, but it is vital to discuss as you start falling for the person or are comfortable knowing the right time to discuss. Also pray that God will give you the right time to do so.

It's also vital to establish what things may be hiding in the other person's closet. It's very important to establish when they last had a boyfriend or girlfriend. If they are fresh out of a relationship; be very careful that you are not being used on the rebound. If they still have a broken heart they need a friend to help them heal not to dive into another relationship immediately.

Maybe something that is hiding in their closet is that they were open to dating a married man and walked down that path. Be very careful in such a situation. You will need to establish whether they recognized it was wrong and that they now do so and would never go down that path again. I've heard the excuse of one of these "predators" who were married and had no qualms of pursuing another woman when they would say to the woman contemplating leaving them, "I will leave my family for you." As a guy, I just think it's crazy how some women fall for such a line. But why do I and probably many other guys recognize this? It is because as men we are analytical. Therefore if a guy will say that to one woman to get her to stay, then even if he kept to his promise, what would happen when he became bored of the new marriage, and met someone more appealing to him? It is most likely the predator would do the same and say "I will leave my family for you" to the new woman in his life.

I use the term "predator", because such men pick on the vulnerable and hide the fact that they are married. In return sadly the woman goes more by feelings and when she hears that he is prepared to leave his family for her she mistakenly feels special and loved. She does not realize that he is just saying what he knows she wants to hear.

WHAT NOT TO DISCUSS WITH YOUR GIRLFRIEND

I'm sure brothers you've wondered what the ladies do in the comfort room or toilet. In other words, why they spend what seems like hours, and sometimes is, after a movie, lol. Or why do they have to go into the bathroom like it's the movie *Noah's Ark*, two by two's.

I can alleviate your curiosity from one of these. I have it via good authority that they will have a conference and discuss the movie in there. "OMGeee!" I hear you gasp. "They are only going to discuss it endlessly outside there anyways, so why not kill two birds with one stone?" Actually they are because they are so excited after the movie they want to discuss it with their fellow "Venusites" (remember woman are from Venus) and they want to relieve their bodies of the vast amounts of Coke they have just drunk during the movie and squirmed in their seats especially if the movie was long as their bladders started to burst. Hahaha.

A gripe I have with the ladies is when they ask two questions in one sentence or one breath. I'm about to answer the first question and they throw in the second before the poor guy, me, has a chance to respond. Moreover the second question is actually superfluous if they give me the chance to respond. For example, a lady will say "Did you like the movie, or did you not?"

What some ladies are notorious for, or maybe most is that they will say to us men, "I'm just going to go into the shop and buy one thing." Guys, grab a magazine or start listening to music on your cell phone, because more often than not, the lady will find more things to do in that one shop. I had to laugh so hard when my best friend and I went shopping in New Zealand with our other flatmate. Just after we were waiting outside of the second-hand store for about 5 minutes he started complaining. If only he had been with us when my flatmate said that she just wanted one thing from the shop and 30 minutes later we exited the store, lol. So guys, be prepared that it will take longer, than just a short visit to the shop, lol.

Another thing with the ladies is that us guys try to be generous when they are trying to plan a meeting time. So if they say "I will just have a rest for 30 minutes" and then you reply generously "Take 45 minutes". Then they flash at you the powefully disarming smile and say "OK, 1 hour". Sometimes it's like, give them a yard and they take a mile. But if we did the same thing we would be scolded, lol.

Maybe this part of the chapter should be written in invisible ink so the ladies don't get to read what I just wrote. Don't forget men, the lady in your life, if she gets hold of this book will start to quiz you on what you have learnt as well as what you have forgotten. Her super-brain will enable her to pull out this information at will, while your brain folder has long discarded it. It has been archived, lol. Sometimes this comes in great help to us guys but often it's really crazily frustrating! Oops, another reason for part of this chapter to be top secret!

Another thing guys, when it comes to movies and life in general always have tissues in your pocket or in your car, because you never know when the waterworks will start. In other words women are emotional beings, sometimes too emotional, but that's also something that endears us to them. They will laugh with us and even cry for us at times.

But remember that God designed us differently, sometimes like different species, but that also means we are compatible and makes the chase even more interesting and funny at the same time. The chase becomes more exciting and rewarding.

Notes

1. Brendan Roberts. *Crusades Rediscovered: In the Light of Human Sexuality and Our Creator* (Kiwi Graphix, Auckland, 2014), 252.

Chapter 5

SHATTERED HEART TO EMBRACING CHRIST

Back in 2010 I fell in love. Well I think I fell in love. I was grinning from ear to ear and pinching myself to see if it was really true that I had a girlfriend after waiting for so long.

She was very beautiful. She had long hair, full lips and her personality was great! She was compassionate, very funny, spontaneous, down to earth and a great dancer. I was amazed by her generous heart. She would even give away her brand new clothes after just wearing them once. We had become very good friends quickly. It took several months to actually start to fall for her. I just really valued our friendship and was really grateful for that. Over time I wanted more.

Going back further into the past, before she was my girlfriend I actually pursued her over the Tasman Sea to Australia. Just one or two days before she was going I secured permission to help chaperone her and her friends. I contacted my sister and she was only too happy to host me. So I booked my plane ticket on-line and excitement filled my heart.

In Australia I romanced her. Our first kiss was on the balcony of the apartment that she and another friend rented for the week. There was a plastic chair on the balcony and before we kissed I asked her if she was sure. This was the moment I had been waiting for. The chair suddenly cracked. But sadly she didn't agree to be my girlfriend. We also had such a romantic time kissing on the beach on the Sunshine Coast. She even jokingly signed her surname as "Roberts" in a guest register in a tourist shop. I bought a chocolate designed as a flower and even chased a naughty bird down the beach screaming at it until it dropped the bright red covered chocolate flower. Hahhaha, what a sight I would have been!

But she didn't want a proper relationship with me; she wanted to remain single as she had just broken up with her boyfriend.

Returning to New Zealand she told me to cool it and that she wanted to remain single, enjoy life and just remain friends with me. I was absolutely crushed. You should see my passport photo. I look not just dejected, but heart-broken. I look like my heart has been run over by a steamroller — it sure felt like it. But that would be almost nothing compared to what was coming.

A few weeks later I flew to another city in New Zealand, Christchurch. After time apart she met me at the airport leaping into my arms and gave me a big passionate kiss. This was the day that she finally agreed to be my girlfriend.

We had our ups and downs in our short relationship. One day I was trying to get her to communicate to me what was troubling her. But she just sat on the park bench in front of the ocean silent. You could have cut the tension with a knife. It took a drive to another spot, silent prayer from both of us asking God to help us to sort this tension out and then a question from me for her to open up. Our relationship almost ended there.

At the beginning I said I think I fell in love. Yes I wanted to marry her, but she wanted to wait three years before getting married. But I was also immature and was in love with the feeling of being in love. Does that sound strange? I was attached to her in the sense that I was reluctant to give her freedom. If she was traveling overseas with friends I wanted to be there? On her birthday she celebrated it without me and I was so distraught and felt so rejected that I cried myself to sleep and woke up later still with wet eyes. In hindsight, I doubt that it was real love between us, but more longing so much to be in love that I loved the feelings I was experiencing. As for my girlfriend, her side of love, was that she said "I love you" to me. You will read whether she really meant it by what is coming.

The next argument we would have would be much worse. I took my girlfriend to the music band, U2. It was my first live concert of such a major band. Yes, it would be one experience I would remember for a long time. I invited two friends along. One of whom was actually more sarcastic and sillier than me, lol. The other was my best friend. The first performance to open the night was J.Z. My girlfriend screamed, "I love you J.Z.!" I was so astonished and even a bit hurt. She could say those words so freely to someone she doesn't even really know when it took several weeks to say the same words to me. Yes it was silly of me to be hurt. During the night I tried to kiss her, especially when it fitted with the words of the song, but she didn't like it. We hugged, but that was it.

I was confused because although she had told me before that she didn't like public displays of affection one day when we attended a weekday Mass at the sign of peace she kissed me on the lips. I was really surprised. She said, "Aren't I allowed to kiss my boyfriend?"

Also during the U2 concert she had averted her eyes from looking into my eyes. She had already told me that she didn't like looking into my eyes because I was "irresistible". But especially at that insecure time of my life I needed eye contact and affection.

The concert was really spectacular with colorful, flashing lights and amazing sets. Bono was a fantastic performer. My best friend left early. When we were leaving we said goodbye to my other friend and then took the wrong exit. We ended up walking for miles. I'm sure it would have taken almost 1.5 – 2 hours in the early morning to find my car.

Driving her back to her house, we both sat silently in the car. Instead of putting my hand on her leg I either used it for driving or just put one hand on my own leg. Because I was the one always initiating I wanted her to initiate for a change.

When we reached her house, I parked the car. She asked if anything was wrong and I said I was ok. Then unusually she merely kissed me on the cheek. I was so stunned. Normally we would kiss goodnight on the lips. As she got out and walked across the street to the steps of her house I sat fuming. I felt like she had slapped me on the face. I wound down the window and said, "What was that?" She replied "a kiss goodnight". My angry reply was "bull shit" and I drove off into the blackness. Before leaving her on the steps I had seen there was a light on at the top of the stairs so I knew she would be alright. Normally I would wait for her to reach the door and go in before driving home.

I sped away down the street and turned the corner. I kept driving and looked at my cell phone, saying "Please text me! Please text me!" It was a cry for help but of course she couldn't hear me and my phone remained silent. It was a cry from my stupid actions. The next day I waited until later in the day to text her and apologize. I was waiting for her text which didn't come.

She did not reply to my text either. That afternoon I attended a wedding, alone. I watched for, longing for her to come to the reception part of the wedding as she was working. But this turned out to be the end of the relationship as she texted me a day or two later saying it was over and that we should just remain friends.

The princesses reading this may even side with my ex-girlfriend and say I was a jerk and disrespectful. Yes I agree I was. Yet for us guys, this wasn't a capital offense, and if someone truly loves someone you work through these issues. Actually there were several things that led up to that explosive situation, including my faults and also little misunderstandings that my girlfriend kept bottled up until one fatal explosion.

Upon being dumped my heart was completely shattered. I felt so lost. I felt so crushed. My heart felt like it had been run over by a steam roller and it felt like it had been cut into thousands of pieces.

How could I get my heart back? How could I rejoin the pieces? How could I get meaning back into my life and hope? Was all really lost as I felt?

The answer was to run to Jesus. I ran to Him with a renewed passion. I ran to Him for consolation. One of my friends was brilliant in also being there for me at this time, offering to spend time with me as a friend. I clung to God. I love the scripture verse which says "Draw near to God and He will draw near to you (James 4:8)."

Do I have any regrets? I think the answer is obvious. Yes I regret that I lost not only my girlfriend but especially that I lost her friendship. I thought that she was the one that God designed for me. In hindsight I don't think she was or that because of her free will she chose not to really love me despite my faults.

Days later I wrote my ex a handwritten 12 page letter which I had started writing at about 3am. This letter explained my insecurities and asked for her forgiveness. I was going to drop it off at her work. I went to Mass in the morning. Then I was absolutely stunned when I saw her with her ex boyfriend going back from receiving Holy Communion. I watched to see where she went to sit. But she had been standing at the back of the Church. Then during the final song, I said excuse me to my friend and went to the back to approach her. I went up to her, uncertain how she would react.

I asked her ex to forgive me as I had pursued her while they had still been together. Then I asked her to forgive me for my immaturity and for hurting her. She replied, "Forgive me for being immature". To this day I don't know what she meant by her statement. I asked her if I could give her a letter that I had written to her. She went to check with her ex whom when I asked if they were back together she said "secret". She also laughed and joked with me. It felt like we had never broken up. I gave her the letter. Then when saying goodbye I didn't realize that it would be the last time that I would ever see her up to this present day.

Sadly, it took me two years to get over my ex. For those who can move on quickly that's good for you.

But there was something else that limited my moving on. It was no help that I felt God giving me signs that she would come back and that she was the one for me. I even saw the same street sign in another part of the country when I was driving back from a funeral praying, singing in tongues and asking God if we were meant to be together. This street sign was so memorable because we had been driving to a Singles For Christ retreat and I shared with her that God had called me to be a fisher of men. Then suddenly we both saw a street sign on our left saying "Fisher St". So coming back from the funeral I was stunned because I saw the same sign. Another time I was driving and asked God the same question and I saw a fishing boat on my left. Even a close friend of mine had two dreams which I thought represented her. One of them was a woman and I arguing in the back of the Church and that we were reconciling too. But all signs must be discerned well.

But even more importantly I know that our God is an all-powerful God. Nothing is impossible for Him! Therefore He can bring someone of equal match or even better than my ex as my future wife. I love the scripture verse that says: "We know that all things work together for good for those who love God, who are called according to his purpose." (Romans 8:28)

Therefore my faith is in God in forming the right woman for me as I believe marriage is the vocation that God is calling me to.

Chapter 6

SPIRITUAL ATHLETICISM

Athletes put their blood, sweat and tears into achieving the best that they can be. When they are injured they take extra care of their body. When they fail they see where they can improve, and maybe even repent asking teammates for forgiveness.

You are a spiritual athlete. God wants your all. He wants your blood, sweat and tears. Jesus showed us the way. He gave His all. He loved until it hurt and then kept loving. He was rejected by those He loved, including his closest friend, St Peter and His enemies. Just imagine hearing your bestie (best friend) deny even knowing you. You would feel betrayed and it would be as if someone stabbed your heart with a knife and twisted it causing you intense pain.

Jesus gave His blood, sweat and tears. In the Garden of Gethsemane, Jesus was tempted to give up — through His humanity. He knew God's will. He understood that the Father was calling Him to be crucified so viciously. He knew He would be whipped to shreds first. Then He would have to give up every drop of His blood. That is what the Eucharist is. Jesus gives Himself totally, every part of Himself — His Body, Blood, Soul and Divinity.

When you are tempted to give up chasing God or chasing the princess that God has destined for you, remember that God is asking for your all, all or nothing. There is no halfway. Sacred Scripture calls us to be either hot or cold. If we are lukewarm, then God will spit us out of His mouth. Of course we should be hot, on fire for God. There are periods where we may feel cold and even that God is so distant from us. That is the time when we need to draw on God's grace even more, like the reserve strength of an athlete; so we push on, having faith and great hope in God's promises to us. He loves us so much: His love and mercy is everlasting.

Why do men especially forget that we are called to take care of ourselves spiritually? We are called to be spiritual athletes and warriors. Why do we take great care of our bodies, going running or doing weights at the gym several times a week, accumulating several hours over a week but neglecting our spiritual lives?

Sadly so many people give God just one hour a week. God desires much more. God thirsts for us. He is calling us to spend more time with Him. Therefore we need to set time aside daily to pray — to listen to Him and to respond, as well as interceding for others. And we need to set time aside daily to read His word as well as study our Catholic faith. I have other books and writings to help you study your faith.

God is waiting in the tabernacle of your local Church or your local adoration chapel with abundant graces ready to bestow on you. Run to Him, surrender everything and receive His graces with an open heart. Then walk the thrilling, life-changing plan that He has destined for you.

The Catechism of the Catholic Church says: "This mystery, then, requires that the faithful believe in it, that they celebrate it, and that they live from it in a vital and personal relationship with the living and true God. This relationship is prayer.[1]

https://pixabay.com/en/girl-praying-hands-eyelashes-15599/

Like any relationship it must be developed; we must spend time and effort for it to be able to grow. Some of our relationships with others are acquaintances, some are good friends, close friends and even best friends or lovers. We are called to a personal relationship with Christ which will develop into best friends and even lovers. This may sound strange, but if as Sacred Scripture tells us God is love then we are called to love God with all we are, our whole being.

How can we develop our personal relationship with Christ? We can do this with a variety of tools. Firstly it is vital to develop such a relationship with prayer.

Tips For Prayer

Preparation
Know what time you have set aside for prayer, pick a scripture passage beforehand and reflect briefly.

Place
Be alone, in a place where you will be uninterrupted and be able to respond to God's presence.

Posture
Our bodies connect with our spirit. Find a way of relaxing and becoming peaceful. If we lie down or pray in bed – it's quite possible that we will just fall asleep!

Presence of God
Be consciously aware of God, intentionally invite God into your life and prayer time and acknowledge His presence.

Passage of Scripture
Read slowly and thoughtfully (possibly twice). Notice any words or ideas or feelings that stir up in you… begin your conversation with God.

You might like to note down places and times that you find really work for your prayer time.[2]

So often we are tempted to give up in our walk with the Lord. We are tempted to give up on His promises to us. He may have placed a dream on our heart and because it takes so long to come to fruition we give up. Because it hurts waiting for the woman God has destined for us, we give up trusting Him. Because we focus on the pain of the suffering we are currently experiencing we give up.

It's like the very inspirational movie, "Facing the Giants". An American Football coach of a school league at his lowest moment, when he was in utter despair, turns to God. As a result he proposes a new team philosophy to his team which had lost so many games it was on the bottom of the championship table: football was just one of the tools to honor God.

Coach challenges his team: "So far it's been about us, how we can win, how we can get the glory. The more I can read this book (the Bible) the more I realize life is not about us. We are not here just to get glory, make money and die. The Bible says God put us here for Him, to honor Him. Jesus said the most important thing you can do with your life is to love God with everything you are and love others as yourself... We need to give the best in every area. If we win we praise Him and if we lose we praise Him. Either way we honor Him with our actions and our attitudes."

When team members were discussing their next match up, one player Brock said their opponents were a lot stronger than them. This made coach give him a lesson of attitude by challenging him to a death crawl; he had to carry a player on his back while crawling with his knees off the ground. He just used his hands and feet to crawl.

Coach asked Brock to give his absolute best. Brock asked if he would be going to the 30 yard line. Coach replied that he thought he could go to the 50 yard line. Brock replied "I can go the 50 if nobody is on my back."

"I think you can do it with Jeremy on your back. Even if you can't I want you to promise me you will do your best."

Brock agrees to give his best. Then coach blindfolds Brock so he won't give up at a certain point where he can go further.

Brock starts strong with much gusto. Coach walks beside him encouraging him. Then as Brock continues he asks coach, "Am I at the 20 yet?"

"Forget the 20. Give me your best!"

Brock continues and breathes in and out loudly as he struggles. Coach says, "Don't quit 'til you got nothing left!"

"It hurts!" Brock complains as he continues.

"I know it hurts! You keep going, you keep going!"

"He's heavy!"

Coach gets down on all fours next to Brock encouraging him to continue: "Keep going! Do not quit on me!" coach urges.

Brock cries out in agony, "It burns!!!"

Coach crawls next to him screaming for him to give his best.

"It's hard!" Brock screams in agony.

"Yes it's hard. You promised me your best, your very best! Don't stop, keep going! 20 more steps! 20 more! Don't quit! Don't quit!"

Coach keeps on screaming at Brock not to quit on him. Then he yells, "10 more steps, 10 more! Keep going, don't quit!"

Brock struggles on and then screams, "I can't do it!"

"You can! You can! 5 more, 5 more! Don't quit! Don't quit!...2 more, 2 more! 1 more!"

Brock collapses. Laying on the ground gasping for breath and seemingly defeated he says, "I don't have any more!"

"Look up Brock. You're in the end zone." Coach replies. Brock had carried someone on his back for the whole length of the football field.

"You are the most influential player on this team. If you walk around defeated, so will they!" Coach challenges Brock. "Don't tell me that you can't give more than I have been seeing. You just carried a 140 pound man across the field. I need you! God has gifted you with the ability of leadership. Don't waste it!"

God is coach in your life. He encourages you and screams at you passionately, urging you to give your best! Jesus is down on His hands and knees, crawling beside you, urging you not to give up. At times in your life you say, "I can't do it!" But Jesus replies, "You can! You can! I know you can! I believe in you!"

Also when you are tempted to give up, reflect on the times that you have succeeded in the past. Maybe you can consider this poem as an inspiration. Remember that God loves you beyond measure and you can ask friends to pray for you:

An Act Of Unselfishness
© Brendan Roberts

Temptation surrounds you.
It's so hard not to give in;
You know that it's wrong,
But anxiety rips at your heart.
You feel depressed;
Gloom seems to devour you.
Suddenly it lifts and disappears.

Once again you thank God,
For your life, family and friends.
You think it's your strength,
That suddenly brought you out of despair.

But low and behold someone said a prayer;
Your friend's act of unselfishness,
Touched the heart of God.

Notes

1. John Paul II. *Catechism of the Catholic Church* (Homebush, NSW: St Pauls, 1995), n. 2558.
2. Father Frank Bird: *Tips on Prayer* as cited in Catholic Bigmag, Issue 2 (free on-line Catholic Magazine) Used with permission.

Chapter 7

LISTEN LORD, YOUR SERVANT IS SPEAKING

Let's admit it, we men aren't always the greatest listeners. I'm sure there will be a few women who will laugh at that statement and say it is greatly under-stated. Maybe we aren't wired the same way in our brains as the ladies. Often they can have ten or more conversations, including one with themselves (joke) at once at the speed of light and retrieve thoughts out of nowhere. We are often reminded, "Remember when you said this?"

But in comparison what we said has often been consigned to oblivion, put into the folder of our brains with instructions, "Do not retrieve because it's not important", lol. So it can take some coaxing until that memory flies from the folder back into our consciousness. Women really are super-humans when it comes to utilizing the powers of the brain. Ok, some men may say aliens, but I'll stick with super-humans, lol. Remember women are from Venus. Not to mention generally they have a greater ability to multi-task.

We men, often need the woman to slow down her speaking, but leave her to her rapid brain activity and keep quiet while we analyze what she is saying. We don't generally read between the lines as much and don't even pretend to know what they are thinking. Ladies, please note that it is virtually impossible to know what a guy is thinking, unless you're his twin or you have been married to him for decades and so can read his expressions that go with his thoughts.

Ladies often think that a guy is lying when he says that he is thinking of nothing. True, sometimes he may say that he was thinking of nothing instead of saying, "I thought you have put on weight in that dress", "You really shouldn't have eaten the entire chocolate bar at once" or "Is that really a mustache on your lip?" lol.

But truly there are times when our brains pause, and rejuvenate as we don't think of anything at all. Guys, I've noticed women will say they are thinking of nothing in order to cover up what they were actually thinking. They are always thinking of something. They don't want to share the thought because it might embarrass them or make them vulnerable. So women use the same logic on us men, that we are always thinking of something.

As men we need to learn the art of listening. I hear a chorus of women yelling their agreement and I'm sure they are dancing that a man has admitted it, lol. We often need to interject in a conversation because it's really hard for us to first make the mental note and keep listening, and two to be able to retrieve the mental note at a moment's notice. We may grunt in affirmation or say "Yes" as we agree to show we are at least trying to listen. We really should get an award for doing this, lol.

As part of the skill of listening we should repeat part of what the other person is saying as women do to show they really are listening. So there must be a balance between too many interjections and listening with no interjections. We men should have a quota of interjections per conversation to help us until we need less, lol.

This skill comes in perfect for listening to God. Often we come to God with all our problems and requests. God has big shoulders and a much bigger heart. But first He wants you to come to Him, quieten your heart and listen to Him.

"Listen Lord, your servant is speaking." Are these the words we tend to speak to God when it comes to our call? Do we tend to tell God what to do rather than listening to what He is trying to say to us? Are we prepared to submit to His will whatever it is?

When it comes to the call of God in our lives we must first of all listen. God can speak to us in a variety of ways. He speaks to us through His living word, Sacred Scripture. He also speaks to us through liturgy, especially the sermon given by the priest if we are awake, lol. Other ways we can hear Him is through other people and through stillness or silence.

God longs for us to spend time with Him, including in silence. God thirsts for us. Jesus waits for us to come to Him in adoration of the Blessed Sacrament which Cardinal Arinze says is the continuation of the Mass. It is the continuation because Christ is really and substantially present in the Eucharist which is reserved for adoration.

Are we afraid of silence? Are we afraid to pray in silence because we may have to face ourselves? Or are we afraid because we think we will get bored? Practice adoring the Lord in periods of silence. Start with five minutes and build it up. In this technological age where we want everything to be given instantly, now, we hate waiting. But God calls us to have patience. As you know patience is a virtue.

Let us practice this virtue through prayer. First say to God, "Come Holy Spirit" or "Veni Sancte Spiritus". Then silence your heart and thoughts. Don't worry if you are distracted. God delights that you want to spend time with Him and have given Him time. After a period of silence open up your Bible and start reading.

You can ask God to speak to you and then Scripture dip, whereby you open the Bible and choose a random part of Scripture to read. Or you can read one or two chapters a day. Also search the internet for quotes from Saints (Google saint quotes) that you could reflect on or listen to the wisdom from the talks of Archbishop Fulton Sheen (see www.fultonsheen.com). We need to feed our souls with good things and so become more attuned to the voice of God.

St Mary McKillop said that we should listen to the voice of God whispering to our hearts. So we need to be unafraid of silence. We need to welcome silence at times. We might be driving to work, and turn off the radio and say hello to the Lord. Or maybe we are on the bus going to study and we have the time to say hi to Jesus. It's also a great opportunity to read His living word. When we make ourselves vulnerable by reading His word publicly we can be a witness to others even if it might embarrass us. Do we really mind being embarrassed by admitting that we love our Lord?

So put some time into your spiritual fitness and you will undoubtedly be delighted by the results. Practice the virtues of prudence (wisdom), humility, kindness, chastity, fortitude (not giving up), charity (self-sacrifice for others) and patience. The more we practice those virtues the more we become like Christ. In fact we become who we are called to be and are more fully human as a result. Thus guys, you are more fully a man by being the image of Christ; and ladies you are more fully a woman by being the image of Christ. In being the image of Christ we are also called to be salt and light to the world.

The Catechism of the Catholic Church (CCC) succinctly explains these virtues. The Cardinal virtues are: prudence, justice, fortitude and temperance. These are called cardinal because they are "hinges" on which the other virtues hang.

Prudence is the "virtue that disposes practical reason to discern our true good in every circumstance and to choose the right means of achieving it."[1] In other words "the prudent person looks where he or she is going (Proverbs 14:15)." St Thomas Aquinas calls it "right reason in action." Through this virtue "we apply moral principles to particular cases without error and overcome doubts about the good to achieve and the evil to avoid."[2]

Justice is the moral virtue through which one has the "firm will to give their due to God and neighbor."[3] It means one should respect the rights of people and "to establish in human relationships the harmony that promotes equity with regard to persons and the common good."[4] Thus one must have uprightness of conduct towards one's neighbor.

Fortitude is the moral virtue that "ensures firmness in difficulties and constancy in the pursuit of good."[5]

It strengthens one's resolve to resist temptations and overcome struggles in the moral life.

Temperance is the moral virtue that "moderates the attraction of pleasures and provides balance in the use of created goods."[6] It ensures that one's will masters "instincts and keeps desires within the limits of what is honorable. The temperate person directs the sensitive appetites toward what is good and maintains a healthy discretion."[7] The Old Testament depicts this through the passage, "Do not follow your base desires, but restrain your appetites." (Sirach 18:30)

Yes we will miss the mark when it comes to the virtues. But no athlete succeeds without failure. Every athlete needs to taste defeat before he or she tastes success. Jesus' closest friends failed Him; all but one ran away when He needed them the most. So, when we fail we must admit what we did was wrong, go to the Sacrament that Our Lord gave us, Reconciliation and humbly ask Him to forgive us through the priest who has the authority of Christ, *in persona Christi.* Therefore the priest does not forgive us but Christ does so as He operates through the priest. After being battered and seeking the Lord's forgiveness we are to get back to our feet and continue the race to heaven willingly and joyfully. But this race does not mean we leave others behind, but that we all get there together and simultaneously.

How would our Church look like if we had the attitude of the U.S. military? Well, what I've seen in some war movies is, "We leave no one behind!" Would we not be more patient, understanding, charitable, kind, chaste, strong – persistent, resilient and self-sacrifice our time, money and talents for others? Would we not seek to be the image of Christ more?

Let us seek to transform our lives through the grace of Christ. First let us savor silence. Let us learn to welcome and embrace silence through the stillness of our hearts. In the Old Testament God was not in the noise but in the stillness. So practice with patience stilling yourself in the Lord's presence. Let Him speak to you by saying "Speak Lord, your servant is listening." Then listen to the whisper of God's love to your heart. God longs for you to delight yourself in His presence. "Call to me and I will tell you of wonderful things I have in store for you (Jeremiah 33:3)."

Notes:

1. John Paul II. Catechism of the Catholic Church (Homebush, NSW: St Pauls, 1995), n. 1806.
2. Ibid.
3. Ibid., n. 1807.
4. Ibid.
5. Ibid., n. 1808.
6. Ibid., n. 1809.
7. Ibid.

Chapter 8

DO REAL MEN GO TO CHURCH?

Before I attempt at answering this question let us explore why many men to the chagrin of the ladies do not attend Church.

There are bound to be many suggestions you as my readers can put forward. For example, there's no beer served at Church, or no cable is available to watch their favorite sports show such as the basketball league or as in the Philippines sitting on the edge of the seat, gripped by the boxing legend Manny Pacquiao. In the Catholic Church the only food served is Holy Communion and it's so small and thin. There is also the common response that many men find the sermons boring. Maybe they are afraid they will fall asleep in the front row which they were dragged into by their spouse and then start snoring like a cow on heat, lol.

After posting in Facebook I received a variety of answers. These include:

- Some are just too busy earning a living for their family. Others don't see the essence in going to church.
- Some may be because of culture. They think that going to Church is for women and old people. It is also because of parents who did not teach their children the importance of attending Church activities.
- Many think it will lessen their manhood.
- Most of them don't really know who God is and the importance of giving Him worship. Cause if they know how great God is, there will be no excuses in not going to church. I guess they should first find God in their lives.
- When you have lots of sand, it is easy to go to the beach, but when you have just a few grains, it is not merely pleasure.

Since I go to church I have fallen ill, I have lost practically all friends, I am isolated, I do not have a job, my family is far from me, but I still go. I have the opportunity to lecture and to give communion, but that is not the point, I think I go because God wants me there and that is fairly enough. It is one place where I can find mercy and peace.

- Unfortunately some men think that praying and going to church is not a cool thing to do. Thinking that it may lessen their masculinity they forget that attending the Holy Mass and praying will prove that they are man enough to stand firm for their faith.
- Busy working to provide for their families.
- Lack of due central emphasis on the sanctity and Real, Substantial Presence of the Incarnate God, Jesus Christ, in the Blessed Sacrament, both in catechesis (leading to ignorance) and in liturgical practice (side-lining of the Tabernacle, and communal lack of reverence in the Presence).
- Basically an upside-down world view, in which we essentially say "we must become greater, He must become less" (See vs. John 3:30).
- I'm sure there are numerous factors, among which social, cultural and intellectual milieu often play a great part, but I think the above is the principal reason. The Real, Substantial Presence is like the anchor, without which one's faith and practice will inevitably fall prey to various waves in the rough seas, but with which they can survive the toughest battering.
- There is a lack of formation, catechesis, and ignorance of the faith. Plus the thing you said about social, cultural, and intellectual milieu! Studying theology and philosophy and history of the Church is crucial to understanding the Faith.
- Because most people lack the very foundation of faith — God's words through the Bible.
- Through misinformation and misconception, and the fruit is to perceive that church–going is corny, useless, feminine, etc.
- In the Bible, it is men that should take the lead, like the father as the head of the family. It is very important that men in the society are properly evangelized according to

the Bible. If a man has the right knowledge then his wife will follow him together with the rest of his household.

If you want to observe men who actually really want to be at the church both physically and spiritually then often it's those that make an effort to turn up to church early, volunteer to actually serve in some capacity at the Mass such as an Extra-ordinary Minister of Holy Communion (Eucharistic Minister) or Lector (reader) or part of the choir.

While there could be some creative ways to draw men to Mass, for example, free barbecue following the Mass, the Church does not force anyone kicking and screaming to go to Mass. I know parents force their kids and that's the parents' role to bring their children up loving God and being fed spiritually. However, the Church respects the free will of men and proposes that they come to the Mass. But what are men who don't go to Church really missing out on?

Before we explore that, there is one way of inviting people that is the focus of many other denominations such as the Evangelical Churches: at the end of their church service they encourage their members to bring someone with them to the next service. This is very rare in the Catholic Church. Because of our baptism we are called to go and make disciples of all nations. What are we afraid of as Catholics? Are we afraid if we invite someone to the Mass they won't like it? You will never know until you actually invite someone. I have been pleasantly surprised how touched friends have been who accepted my invitation to come with me to Mass.

So what is it that men really are missing out on when they don't go to Mass? I don't mean just sitting there and wishing they were not there, lol. I actually mean what are they missing when they do not participate in the Mass with their body and soul?

For the answer to this question let us re-look at God's love letter to men:

Run to me I'm waiting for you. Don't feed your ego. Feed your soul with my living word and my Body, the living Bread. I not only want to sustain, nourish and purify your soul, I want you to be transformed and to be a living image of me.

No matter what you have done in the past, I love you. I'm waiting for you to come into my presence, to fall to your knees before the Blessed Sacrament and to receive the bountiful graces I want to lavish upon you.

God is calling us to feed our souls both with His living word daily and His living Bread, His Body and His Blood. The Eucharist is what differentiates us Catholic and Orthodox Christians from other Christians. The Eucharist is the "life, source and summit of our faith".[1]

The Early Christians, whom we call the Early Church Fathers, have also revealed how magnificent the Holy Eucharist is for us. St Ignatius calls the Eucharist the "medicine of immortality". This links in perfectly with Sacred Scripture and Jesus saying that those who eat His Body and drink His Blood have eternal life and He will also raise them up on the last day:

> "Those who eat my flesh and drink my blood have eternal life, and I will raise them up on the last day, for my flesh is true food and my blood is true drink. Those who eat my flesh and drink my blood abide in me, and I in them." (John 6:54-56)

So back to the question: what are men missing out on when they don't go to Mass? They are actually missing out on the self-gift of Jesus Christ through Holy Eucharist. They are missing out on the intimate uniting with Jesus when He gives Himself totally to us, freely and unreservedly — He gives us His Body, Blood, Soul and Divinity. So as St Peter tells us we thus share in Christ's divinity (see 2 Peter 1:3-4). That's why John 6:54 says "those who eat His Body and drink His Blood have eternal life". That alone should be motivation enough for us men to go to Mass.

ALL FOR ONE AND ONE FOR ALL

God is asking men (and women too) for total commitment. Could it be that some men are afraid to commit themselves to God? Could it be that they think they will have to turn away from things that they enjoy?

God is calling all men (yes women too) to love His living word! Men, we are called to read and study God's word, and to live it. Yes it's so hard! Yes it's challenging to one's ego! Yes it is life changing and will make you better lovers of your wives and your children.

I've also heard men say they don't want to go to Church because they don't want to be judged or because it is full of hypocrites. But I could tell that such statements showed that the very same person was judging the others in the Church by saying it was full of hypocrites. Yes the Church is full of sinners. St John in his letter makes it clear that we are all sinners when he says:

> If we say that we have no sin, we deceive ourselves, and the truth is not in us. If we confess our sins, he who is faithful and just will forgive us our sins and cleanse us from all unrighteousness. If we say that we have not sinned, we make him a liar, and his word is not in us (1 John 1:8).

God's word talks about such a relationship with God. We are called to love the Lord our God with all our mind, heart and soul and our neighbor as ourselves (See Matthew 22:27). When it comes to being lukewarm Sacred Scripture is very clear.

> I know your works; you are neither cold nor hot. I wish that you were either cold or hot. So, because you are lukewarm, and neither cold nor hot, I am about to spit you out of my mouth. For you say, "I am rich, I have prospered, and I need nothing." You do not realize that you are wretched, pitiable, poor, blind, and naked (Revelation 3:16).

So my fellow brothers, let us not be lukewarm but seek God with all our very beings. Let us seek to make Him number one in our lives and to let the love from that relationship flow out to others. No matter what your past is you can make a new beginning today! You can allow God to change the path your life is now taking. You can allow God to surprise you with the most amazing life you will ever be able to live.

God is calling us to be on fire for Him. His desire is that we are hot, not lukewarm. He wants us to passionately serve Him and spread His love to the wider world. What an amazing opportunity we have to spread the Gospel when we have social media at our fingertips.

Notes:

1. Vatican II. Lumen Gentium, n. 11.

Chapter 9

THE POOR CAPTURED MY HEART

Beloved, let us love one another, for love is from God, whoever loves has been born of God and knows God. (1 John 4:7)

When it comes to helping the poor a lot of thoughts assail us. We say they should really be helping themselves, that they are lazy. Can we really help so many people? Therefore when we walk down the street like the Jewish Priest in the parable of the Good Samaritan we cross the street and divert our gaze or mentally we do that when we divert our focus from the outstretched hand and the pleading eyes, which are looking for hope.

It is a very good habit to give the poor food. However if we don't have the time to buy food then we should give them some change. The week following Pope Francis' visit to the Philippines it tore my heart to see people walking past a blind beggar. He smiled when I not only gave him money but defended him and advocated for him by urging people to give to him. But they just looked at me and then kept on walking. Another time here in the Philippines I came across a beggar. I not only gave him some small change, but when I noticed the filthy state of his hands I was walking away and knew I had something else to do for him. I reached into my pocket, stopped, turned around and approached him. He was grateful as I poured hand sanitizer/cleaner into his hands so he could clean them.

Sacred Scripture is very clear when it comes to how often we should give to beggars: "Give to everyone who begs from you (Matthew 5:42)."

If everyone, or just a lot more people, gave a little to beggars on the street then they would be cared for and would not have to struggle as much. What a vicious cycle it is not to eat healthily or be able to care for oneself with dental care or be able to visit the doctor when you need to, but only get worse not better.

Pope Francis, in the *Joy of the Gospel* also urges us to help the poor. He speaks of a "commitment to the poor"[1] with making the Church constantly going outside of herself. He also quotes St John Chrysostom regarding the poor: "Not to share one's wealth with the poor is to steal from them and to take away their livelihood. It is not our own goods which we hold, but theirs".[2]

We are called to be generous now, rather than waiting to be financially secure. As we bless others God will bless us.

The reason why I first visited the Philippines was to regain a heart for the poor. This I did when I witnessed so many poor in the country and especially when with members of CFC Singles For Christ we visited a poor village in Cagayan de Oro being supported by our community. It was here a mother deeply touched our hearts when she shared that she and her children only had a type of rice porridge to eat once a day. Her husband was away working in Manila. He would send money home periodically. But when he did return home to visit he would spend most of the time spending their money on alcohol and was drunk.

We are also called to "small daily acts of solidarity in meeting the real needs which we encounter."[3] The word "solidarity" refers to "something more than a few sporadic acts of generosity. "It presumes the creation of a new mindset which thinks in terms of community and the priority of the life of all over the appropriation of goods by a few."[4]

Pope Francis says that we should always remember that the planet belongs to all mankind. Then he says that because some people are born in places with fewer resources or less development it does not justify the fact that they are living with less dignity. It must be reiterated that "the more fortunate should renounce some of their rights so as to place their goods more generously at the service of others".[5]

Pope Francis says we as Christians are called always with the help of our pastors to hear the cry of the poor. He then quotes the bishops of Brazil who plead for the landless, homeless and those lacking food and health care:

> Seeing their poverty, hearing their cries and knowing their sufferings, we are scandalized because we know that there is enough food for everyone and that hunger is the result of a poor distribution of goods and income. The problem is made worse by the generalized practice of wastefulness.[6]

God shows the poor "his first mercy"[7]. Inspired by this, the Church has made an option for the poor which is understood as a "special form of primacy in the exercise of Christian charity, to which the whole tradition of the Church bears witness".[8]

Quoting Pope Benedict XVI Pope Francis emphasizes that God "became poor for us, so as to enrich us with his poverty".[9]

Then Pope Francis says why he wants a Church which is poor and for the poor:

> They have much to teach us. Not only do they share in the sensus fidei [sense of faith], but in their difficulties they know the suffering Christ. We need to let ourselves be evangelized by them. The new evangelization is an invitation to acknowledge the saving power at work in their lives and to put them at the center of the Church's pilgrim way. We are called to find Christ in them, to lend our voice to their causes, but also to be their friends, to listen to them, to speak for them and to embrace the mysterious wisdom which God wishes to share with us through them.[10]

Thus we are called to appreciate the poor in their goodness. He says: "The love by which we find the other pleasing leads us to offer him something freely".[11] The poor person, when loved, "is esteemed as of great value".[12]

Then Pope Francis challenges us with a wonderful way of engaging anyone, including the poor, with the Gospel: He speaks of a type of preaching which falls to every one of us Christians as a daily responsibility. We are called to bring the Gospel to the people we meet whether they are our neighbors or strangers. He calls it informal preaching which takes place in the middle of a conversation. Thus we are called to be "constantly ready to bring the love of Jesus to others, and this can happen unexpectedly and in any place: on the street, in a city square, during work, on a journey."[13]

In this preaching, which is always respectful and gentle, the first step is personal dialogue, when the other person speaks and shares his or her joys, hopes and concerns for loved ones, or so many other heartfelt needs.

He says it is only after the person has finished sharing that we can bring in God's word. Therefore we should keep quiet and practice the art of listening. He suggests that bringing in God's word is done "perhaps by reading a Bible verse or relating a story, but always keeping in mind the fundamental message: the personal love of God who became man, who gave himself up for us, who is living and who offers us his salvation and his friendship."[14]

He says the message we bestow can be presented directly through "a personal witness or gesture, or in a way which the Holy Spirit may suggest in that particular situation."[15]

He then explains a wonderful way of concluding the preaching:

> If it seems prudent and if the circumstances are right, this fraternal and missionary encounter could end with a brief prayer related to the concerns which the person may have expressed. In this way they will have an experience of being listened to and understood; they will know that their particular situation has been placed before God, and that God's word really speaks to their lives.[16]

Another great reason for why we should be a witness to the poor is as St Teresa of Avila relates we are to be Christ to them:

> "Christ has no body now on earth but yours,
> no hands but yours,
> no feet but yours;
> Yours are the eyes through which to look out Christ's compassion to the world;
> Yours are the feet with which He is to go about doing good;
> Yours are the hands with which He is to bless men now."

"He alone loves the Creator perfectly who manifests a pure love for his neighbor." St Bede the Venerable.

Notes

1. Francis, Joy of the Gospel, n.97.
2. Ibid., n.57; Saint John Chrysostom, De Lazaro Concio, II, 6: PG 48, 992D.
3. Francis, *Joy of the Gospel*, n.188.
4. Ibid.
5. Paul VI, Apostolic Letter, Octogesima Adveniens (14 May 1971), 23: AAS 63 (1971), 418.; Francis, Joy of the Gospel, n.190.

6. Conferência Nacional Dos Bispos Do Brazil, Exigências evangélicas e éticas de superação da miséria e da fome" (April 2002), Introduction, as cited in Joy of the Gospel, n.191.
7. John Paul II, Homily at Mass for the Evangelization of Peoples in Santo Domingo (11 October 1984), 5: AAS; as cited in Francis, Joy of the Gospel, n.198.
8. John Paul II, Encyclical Letter *Sollicitudo Rei Socialis* (30 December 1987), 42: AAS 80 (1988), 572; as cited in Francis, Joy of the Gospel, n. 198.
9. Address at the Inaugural Session of the Fifth General Conference of the Latin American and Caribbean Bishops (13 May 2007), 3: AAS 99 (2007), 450 as cited in Pope, Francis, *Joy of the Gospel*, n.198.
10. Francis, *Joy of the Gospel*, n. 198.
11. Saint Thomas Aquinas, S. Th., I-II, q. 110, a. 1; as cited in Francis, Joy of the Gospel, n.199.
12. Ibid., I-II, q. 26, a. 3; as cited in Francis, *Joy of the Gospel*, n. 199.
13. Francis, *Joy of the Gospel.*, n.127.
14. Ibid., 128.
15. Ibid.
16. Ibid.

Chapter 10

GOD'S LIVING IMAGE

"Run to me I'm waiting for you. Don't feed your ego. Feed your soul with my living word and my Body, the living Bread. I not only want to sustain, nourish and purify your soul, I want you to be transformed and to be a living image of me."

From God's Love Letter

I have had friends who were struggling with their walk with the Lord ask me how they can draw closer to God. The answer is above. God is waiting for us to run to Him. In fact like the *Prodigal Son* parable God is running to us. He loves us intensely and passionately! He actually loves us infinitely. It's so hard to comprehend such a level of intimacy with God.

When we get to heaven God will share the glory, power, beauty, and love of the Holy Trinity with us. Wow! Imagine that! That is what we are longing for, when we will have full knowledge of whom God is, like the angels do. Now we must live by faith, faith in what we don't see. We can see God's effects and we can see that God has revealed Himself through both natural and supernatural revelation.

Sacred Scripture also reveals that as stars have a certain type of glory and shine differently so our resurrected bodies will too shine. (See 1 Corinthians 15:39-58.)

But for now God lets us have a taste of that uniting with the Blessed Trinity; He allows us to unite with His Son through the living word and in a much more unique and eternally deeper way through the Holy Eucharist.

We are called to image Jesus Christ. What does Sacred Scripture say regarding being Jesus' image?

"By this way we may be sure that we are in him: whoever says, 'I abide in him', ought to walk just as he walked (1 Corinthians 2:5-6)."

God's Living Image 153

"And all of us, with unveiled faces, seeing the glory of the Lord as though reflected in a mirror, are being transformed into the same image from one degree of glory to another; for this comes from the Lord, the Spirit (2 Corinthians 3:18).

"A disciple is not above the teacher, nor a slave above the master, it is enough for the disciple to be like the teacher, and the slave like the master. If they have called the master of the house Beelzebul, how much more will they malign those of his household! (Matthew 10:24-25)"

"A disciple is not above the teacher, but everyone who is fully qualified will be like the teacher (Luke 6:40)."

"Little children, let no one deceive you. Everyone who does what is right is righteous, just as he is righteous (1 John 3:7)."

"For to this you have been called, because Christ also suffered for you, leaving you an example, so that you should follow in his steps. 'He committed no sin, and no deceit was found in his mouth (1 Peter 2:21-22)."

"So if I, your Lord and Teacher, have washed your feet, you also ought to wash one another's feet. For I have set you an example, that you also should do as I have done to you (John 13:14-15)."

"You were taught to put away your former way of life, your old self, corrupt and deluded by its lusts, and to be renewed in the spirit of your minds, and to clothe yourselves with the new self, created according to the likeness of God in true righteousness and holiness (Ephesians 4:22-24)."

St Peter gives the ultimate reason for why we should be holy, to be the image of God when he says that God says to us: "You shall be holy, for I am holy (1 Peter 1:16)."

If we seek after holiness, being the image of God, then we are truly living up to who we are called to be, we are indeed man fully alive.

JUST LIVE LIFE TO THE FULLEST

There is one saying which the world has taken and twisted: one should *live life to the fullest*. It is a twist of the Gospel saying of Jesus "I have come, that they may have life and live it to the fullest (John 10:10)." Yet it is the opening for the Gospel. When you hear someone saying that ask them if they know where that saying comes from? Tell them it is actually a saying of Jesus. That true living life to the fullest is found in Him. He offers us the fullness of joy which is long-lasting while the world's joy is often short lived which is blatantly made clear by many in Hollywood who seem to have everything but often have the most dysfunctional and sad lives when they do not have God as the center of their lives.

Do you really want to image yourself on bad examples from Hollywood or do you want to image yourself on the source of true joy, peace, happiness and love? Do you want to image yourself on someone who will show you mainly things on this earth, or do you want to image yourself on someone who will show you the best for living on this earth and prepare you for eternal life? Also God calls us to imitate those who have been our leaders (see Hebrews 13:7). The saints have indeed been our spiritual leaders; they have shown us that we too as humans, though we fail we can repent, get back up and return with passion in loving and serving God and our neighbor.

Here is a reflection I wrote about being the Mirror of Christ.

MIRROR OF CHRIST

Are you a mirror of Christ? Maybe you have cracks and have been dropped a few times. Maybe you feel shattered and worthless. But even if you are the latter Christ calls you to wholeness. Christ calls you to a loving relationship with Him. This relationship through the Church will make you whole again. He is offering His graces to you.

Even if you feel like a broken mirror let others see the splendor and beauty of Christ in the shards. You may have to gather those shards together, for then the beauty will be greater than individual shards scattered from your heart. When others see Christ reflected some will draw near to you. You have the answer for their lives. You have the answer for what they are searching for. They too want meaning and the fullness of Christ in their lives. Once they experience and taste the joy and beauty of Christ they too will want to share and reflect it to others — for thus they have become a mirror of Christ.

For us Catholics and Orthodox, Christ's power through the sacraments heals our broken mirror. There are no more shards or cracks but a beautiful shiny wholeness. Christ can be seen so clearly and for some they are afraid of the view, others ashamed and others drawn to it. Some will hurl rocks because of their fear or shame. Others will shine the mirror with encouragement. There are two great sacraments for keeping this mirror intact: Reconciliation and the Holy Eucharist. The former heals the mirror to its original glory after being broken. The latter heals scratches and even protects from some future scratches.

Let the glory of Christ shine from your mirror. You are the mirror of Christ. Who has been a mirror for you in your life? Maybe they have passed onto the glory of heaven. I have had many examples and of course the saints are wonderful examples such as St Maximilian Kolbe, St Francis Xavier, St Padre Pio, St Teresa of Liseux, St Catherine of Sienna, St John the Disciple, St Brendan of Clonfert, St John Paul II and Blessed Mother Teresa.

Chapter 11

TRANSFORMATION TO GREATNESS

"Transformers, more than meets the eye" chimes through the speakers in the movie theaters or from your T.V. or computer device. You might even admit to singing along to the catchy tune. Or maybe like me after the movie you managed to speak while burping, sounding like Optimus Prime, lol. The drink of coke during the movie helped me achieve such a tremendous feat.

We too are called to transformation. But we do not change from one state to a completely different one. Sadly sometimes often when we sin we go from a greater degree to a lesser degree, from greatness to being even subhuman at times. We are called to transformation to greatness, to the greater degree.

Transformation is a grace of Christ. It is also a choice which precedes the grace. Like the famous robots, because of free will, we can do good or bad. So we must want to become transformed to be more like Christ. But how are we transformed?

Sacred Scripture reveals the answer is that we must have the mind of Christ (1 Corinthians 2:14-16). To do this we must use a variety of tools. This includes knowing more and more what Christ was like by reading the Scriptures.

We can also get to know Christ more through prayer and studying the Catholic faith regarding why the Church teaches certain things. The Church, founded by Christ is united to Christ and so the Church knows Christ intimately as a spouse knows her husband.

Who else would know Christ in-depth? Christ's own mother, Mama Mary, who raised Him as a baby and gave her all to Christ. Our Lady even embraced Him with a mother's tender heart at the foot of the Cross while her own heart was shattered as if struck by the lance that sliced into her Son.

We must not forget St Joseph who would have taught Jesus many of the principles and laws of the Jewish faith. We know it was at least up to when Jesus was lost in the temple.

So we can be transformed through Scripture, prayer, and studying our faith. We can also be transformed through putting our faith into action. For example, instead of just talking about helping others, we reach out to those in need. Instead of being like the Jewish Priest and walking on the other side of the road when we see someone begging, we can offer to buy the beggar some food or if in a hurry give a small donation. Instead of moaning when we do not get our own way, we can take the time to see where the other person is coming from. Instead of hating our enemies we can do what Christ called us to do, love our enemies. Instead of harboring resentment, we can forgive as Christ showed us.

There is another vital method for transformation: frequent reception of the Sacraments. You could say that Christ offers us an antidote to the evil in the world. But this antidote is more powerful than what we can get through medicine because it affects the spiritual realm.

Through the sacraments we receive grace which elevates and heals. These sacraments are life-giving because they mediate the presence and action of God in a unique way.

Grace is also the communication of God's Self which desires our response; we are called to open our hearts to God's will. Therefore we are called to make our own fiat, our own total giving to Christ. We should have the intention that whatever we own is not ours but God's. Also as discussed what we have belongs to the poor, it is not ours but theirs.

Scripture tells us that our own body does not belong to ourselves, but it has been bought for a price and should be used for God's glory (1 Corinthians 6:19-20). So why do we abuse our bodies through taking things that are harmful to it whether it be excessively or for a prolonged period of time?

Our response to God's self-communication can be through forgiving others and at times just as important forgiving ourselves. Sometimes the hardest thing to do is to forgive oneself.

Our response is also to seek to live the virtues such as the cardinal virtues of prudence, justice, temperance (restraint) and courage (fortitude) and the three theological virtues of faith, hope, and love (charity).

When we become more like Christ we are being transformed to greatness. We are actually becoming more fully human because we are becoming the person that God calls us to be. Thus we are called to reach beyond the present to reach our fullest potential. It is a task that God calls us to be persistent at, to continue to work at achieving.

This process of transformation is also known as conversion, which is a life-long process to become more and more like Christ. Holiness is our number one vocation; the vocation which embraces all other vocations.

It is not so scary when we think of holiness as becoming more like Christ rather than falsely seeing it as giving up fun for an unobtainable goal. Christ said that we are called to live life to the fullest in Him (John 10:10). The goal is indeed obtainable as many of us have been witnessed to by people who lived their faith and so practiced what they preached. We will only achieve the fullness of being when we totally share in the divine nature of Christ (See 1 Peter 1:4). This process of divinization is happening through prayer, and especially through receiving the sacraments worthily whereby we receive the grace of Christ with open and grateful hearts and whereby we bear fruits of love and service to others as a result. We share in Christ's divine nature, especially through receiving Holy Communion as we receive his Body, Blood, Soul, and Divinity. We do not become less human, but we become more fully human; we become who we were made and thus destined to be.

They will know we are Christians by our love. We are called to be the light of the world (Matthew 5:14). We receive Christ's love through the Sacraments, especially through the Sacrament of Baptism and Holy Eucharist. When we bear the fruit of the Sacraments, we are loving others and so "God remains in us and his love comes to perfection in us" (1 John 4:13).

St Paul tells us that we are in a spiritual battle. Therefore in order to become more like Christ, as we hear during the distribution of the ashes during Ash Wednesday, we must turn away from sin and be faithful to the Gospel. Also if we resist the Devil he will flee (James 4:7).

We have been given a very powerful prayer by Pope Leo XIII to resist Satan and his demons, the Prayer to St Michael the Archangel. He composed the prayer after being given a vision of the Church in the 20th century which made him collapse.

St Louis de Montfort believes that praying the Holy Rosary is also an effective weapon against Satan. St Alphonsus of Liguori relates the walls of Jericho collapsing to that of the false teachings disappearing after fervent prayer of the Holy Rosary. He says, "The swimming pool of Jerusalem was not as healing for the bodily sick as the rosary is as remedy for the spiritually diseased."

But don't forget receiving the Sacrament of Reconciliation at least once a month, as Blessed Mother Teresa encourages, is also very effective as we are healed, strengthened and raised up through grace.

Like the movie Transformers we are in a battle of good versus evil and good always triumphs. Let us seek to be transformed, to put on the mind of Christ and to become more fully human through our own conversion. Then as we begin to shine with the light of Christ, becoming more like Him we will attract people to see the fullness of life that is offered through our awesome God. In being the image of Christ it is our responsibility to be the witness of the love and mercy of God and the joy of living a life which is the fullness of life in Christ.

Chapter 12

DRINKING FOR PLEASURE OR TO OBLIVION

When it comes to alcohol it is something that can give us pleasure. It warms the stomach and can even relax us. But the key is to always remember to drink in moderation. My ex-flatmate was so funny when it came to reaching her limit. She would start to raise her voice and then snort when laughing. It was hilarious to watch.

While in the process of writing this book I have been staying in Mandaluyong in Manila, Philippines. I started running almost daily and then added to my routine crunches (sit ups). One day I observed a man doing vigorous exercise which included squats. I could see he was very fit. When I was considering approaching him I thought I would try an exercise where you get down on all fours like you are starting a race. Then you move the legs alternately forward. I saw a man on a bench and said hello. He returned my greeting and added, "Your fast!" He had seen me doing laps of the field. First he asked me if I do kick boxing. Then he told me that he coaches the sport.

When we got talking he shared how he had worked on oil tankers and had even visited New Zealand. I found out that he was Catholic. After talking for awhile he raised the subject of temptations. As a man to man conversation this is where it really got interesting.

I said that when it came to temptation we may think we are strong enough to fight it but we should look at how we can avoid it. For example if the internet site is pornographic we should not click on the site or if we really don't trust ourselves then we can Google ways of blocking the porn sites. A friend of mine confessed recently to being addicted to porn sites. I helped him in this process by asking Google. So if you want me to walk through this with you then email me. Another way to fight temptation is not to step in the door of a strip club or turn off the T.V. program if it is bad morally.

When it comes to alcohol we should know our limits or if we have no control because of alcoholism or are under age then we should not drink at all. When we drink excessively it is not us controlling the liquor but the liquor controlling us.

During the Lord's Prayer we pray, "Lead us not into temptation, but deliver us from evil." But what we really practice is the latter where we ask God to deliver us from evil, but lead ourselves into temptation.

My friend raised the common example where one is coaxed to drink by his drinking mates. I said we should know our limit and even pace ourselves. So you can have a shot or two or a glass of beer, and then a glass of water.

Sure we guys can get carried away when we are part of a pack. The group mentality can mean we try to convince our friend to drink some more. But there is a limit to the coaxing. It's called respecting his right to say "no". So if your friends are not concerned for your ultimate happiness and do not respect your right to say "enough", then are they really your true friends?

As men we think we are being a man when we drink excessively because we are coaxed to or dared to. Yes we may be a man, a caveman, lol. We are letting ourselves be tempted to drink to the excess. In fact if we let ourselves run our lives that way, we are probably afraid to go against the flow, to look like a girl. But in reality we are not man enough to resist the temptation and to have the courage to say either "I've had enough for now guys" or "Let me set my own pace boys." Believe it or not, if they just want to drink themselves to oblivion they are just that, boys. A real man will make a stand, even if he will be laughed at. A real man will stand up for what he believes even if he will be ostracized as a result.

Do you really want an empty wallet from drinking excessively? Do you really want the alcohol to control your life and even to control your conscience where you cannot resist anything when wasted by drinking too much?

I enjoy my alcohol, but in moderation. I can drink a cocktail even here in the Philippines. Depending on whether I have eaten or not then I will feel light headed as a result, but I am still in full control of myself.

Another temptation that we men face is the temptation to go from admiring a very beautiful woman to turning her into an object for our gratification.

One day while going for another early morning run here in the Philippines I was sitting on a small wall with my best friend, whose book this is. We had just read the readings of the day from Sacred Scripture. Then as usual we would share our thoughts.

"When I first came here to the Philippines I was so flirty" I said to Elly. She already knew this. But it was going to be the backdrop of my sharing. At the moment when I said "flirty" I looked up. I had heard high heels doing their tap dance on the pavement. My innate manliness responded to the call of the sound of heels, lol.

The sight that greeted me was surreal. This very beautiful woman was right upon us, wearing a very tight body hugging dress with red and black stripes. This is what Elly remembered. I was so afraid the stranger would misinterpret what I had just said. She would have had to be deaf or in another world not to have heard me say "flirty". But she never flinched a muscle of that pretty face. I looked intently at her for her reaction. But there was none. She neither looked at me nor Elly nor never missed a beat in the rhythmic tap dance of her stilettos on the pavement.

Elly burst out laughing and said, "Are you sure, *was* flirty?"

It was as if God sent an angel in hot disguise to make a point. OK, she wasn't a vegetable, but as a creature of God she was a beautiful creation.

I could say that this is one of the funniest things that I have ever witnessed. In fact Elly and I sat there laughing for awhile and recalling what had just unfolded before our startled eyes. But I was the victim! Whoever said God does not have a great sense of humor? I'm sure He was really laughing at the surprise He sprung on me and Elly so that I could include it in this book.

Chapter 13

WHY SURRENDER YOUR ALL?

"Love to be real, it must cost — it must hurt — it must empty us of self." Blessed Mother Teresa.

Are we afraid to give God total control of our lives? Are their areas in our lives which we hold back from God, even ashamed to give to Him?

I heard a sermon recently where it was a story of a little boy who was afraid of water. He wanted to cross a bridge and asked God if he could hold His hand. But the boy was astounded that God said no to his request.

"Why won't you let me hold your hand?" the boy asked?

"Because I want to hold your hand." God answered him.

"But what's the difference?"

"In the storms of life you might become afraid, forget that you are holding my hand and let go and hurt yourself. But if I'm holding your hand I will never let go of your hand. I will never forget you."

God calls us to surrender our hopes, our dreams, our fears, and faults and our sins to Him. He wants us to completely trust in Him and His plan for our life.

But what could keep someone back from surrendering completely to God?

FEELING UNWORTHY

You might think that you are not worthy of God's love because of your past or things you are currently doing. Maybe you think you've done too many mistakes in your life.

But God's answer is "Come to me, all you who are weary and burdened and I will give you rest. Take my yoke and learn from me, for I am gentle and humble in heart, and you will find rest for your souls. For my yoke is easy and my burden is light (Matthew 11:28-30)."

TOO HARD

Maybe you are afraid to surrender all to God because you fear that He will ask you to do something which is beyond your ability that is too hard for you (See 1 Corinthians 10:13). But God will always offer you the grace, the strength to embrace His divine will if you surrender all to Him and seek His grace especially through the Sacraments.

Maybe you have surrendered your all to Christ but your faith journey ended in disappointment. It's important to know that surrendering is not always easy. Often it's very hard but God will equip us with the grace. Jesus Christ reveals how extremely hard it was for Him to surrender to the Father's plan:

> Then going out he went, as was his custom, to the Mount of Olives, and the disciples followed him. When he arrived at the place he said to them, "Pray that you may not undergo the test." After withdrawing about a stone's throw from them and kneeling, he prayed, saying, "Father, if you are willing, take this cup away from me; still, not my will but yours be done."
>
> And to strengthen him an angel from heaven appeared to him. He was in such agony and he prayed so fervently that his sweat became like drops of blood falling on the ground (Luke 22:39-44).

AFRAID OF SUFFERING

Someone may also fear surrendering to God because they are afraid to suffer. God may call us to suffer, but we can also find joy and happiness amidst suffering. If God calls us to suffer we are very blessed because as St Paul says: "We are children of God, and if children, then heirs, heirs of God and joint heirs with Christ — if, in fact, we suffer with him so that we may also be glorified with him (Romans 8:17)."

Some suffering that people go through these days, especially in the poor countries is the desperation to seek work in order to survive. It takes really hard work and even all of one's energy. Many have to work more than one job in order to survive. Thus the path to success seems impossible. Also if someone gets sick while at work and they don't have a sympathetic boss they could be fired. For those who get very sick then the financial strain is enormous. Others suffer greatly because they cannot find employment.

But how are we to handle these situations? Are we to try to cope only in our own strength? Does God really care about us when we have to go through such trials and tribulations? I have written a poem which answers whether God cares:

Where Is God?
© Brendan Roberts

Oh the pain is tormenting;
The anguish too much to bare;
I felt so alone;
robbed, cheated.

Why was someone so dear to me
taken away?
I needed them so;
There was so much I wanted to say.

Now there is only an empty chasm;
Pain raking my heart;
Who really understands me?
Who really cares?

So where is God?
This God of love?
My child, stop and listen;
I care, I am within you.

Yes Jesus cares and He understands. "How could Jesus understand?" you might ask. Jesus experienced far greater suffering than we could even imagine or endure in our own strength. He suffered rejection by most of the religious leaders of the time and even many followers rejected Him when He called them to eat His flesh and drink His blood (See John 6). We know that what He was talking about was His Body and Blood, the Holy Eucharist. But many of His followers could not understand that He could give life through eating His flesh and blood and so left Him refusing to believe in Him.

The holy family of Mary and Joseph and the unborn Jesus (alive in the womb) also understand suffering because they became refugees whereby they had to flee their town at a moment's notice. As refugees they had to suffer the hardships of possible bandits, severe heat in the day and extreme cold at night, including Mary experiencing this while pregnant.

Mama Mary understands what it's like to not know where your next food will be coming from and also not knowing how long one must be a refugee. But her trust was impeccable. Her faith was in God who she knew would take care of her. This doesn't mean that Mary didn't taste fear. Remember that when the angel appeared to Mary in the annunciation he said to her, "Do not be afraid."

Mama Mary understands suffering because she lost Joseph and so had to raise Jesus on her own at some stage in her life. So for those women who are struggling raising children on their own, Mama Mary understands. She also understands suffering as she had to witness her son being crucified unjustly as a criminal. She understands because she held the body of Jesus in her arms.

Suffering can lead us closer to God. It is through other people's love, selflessness, compassion, solidarity and concern that God can be revealed to those who are suffering. Jesus showed us the way because He embraced His own suffering while alleviating the suffering of others.

Secular society tends to believe that embracing suffering is ridiculous. Most people hate to suffer. But it is very much a part of human life. The mother to be undergoes great suffering in order to bear the child of her and her husband's into the world. Once the child is born into the world and the pain ended the mother can rejoice. In fact even amidst suffering we can experience joy. Pope Francis says:

> Joy adapts and changes, but it always endures, even as a flicker of light born of our personal certainty that, when everything is said and done, we are infinitely loved. I understand the grief of people who have to endure great suffering, yet slowly but surely we all have to let the joy of faith slowly revive as a quiet yet firm trust, even amid the greatest distress...The steadfast love of the Lord never ceases, his mercies never come to an end; they are new every morning. Great is your faithfulness.[1]

We can either draw closer to God, giving Him thanks and trusting that everything is in His hands as well as drawing closer to others who are caring for us or we can become bitter towards God and others and withdraw from them.

We can share our suffering with Christ, by offering it up for those who are less fortunate than ourselves, for those who are suffering far worse than us and have lost all hope and for the conversion of the world to Christ.

What does Sacred Scripture say about suffering? In the Old Testament Yahweh (God) often punished those He loved in order to lead them to repentance and thus conversion of heart. The sufferings inflicted by God include an "invitation of His mercy."[2] Thus the loving God disciplined His people, seeking their change of heart. God knew what was best for them. He knew what would lead them to true happiness.

Also there are many examples of the nation of Israel, the Chosen People turning away from God by breaking His covenant which He was always faithful to. But no matter what they did God always called them back to Himself while always remaining faithful. Like a loving parent God had to correct and discipline His people, whom He loved.

To really explore the why of suffering, to dive into the richness of suffering one must look to the revelation of divine love which is the "ultimate source of the meaning of everything that exists."[3]

When we look to the Cross of Christ we see the revelation of divine love. The wider world looks at the Cross and can't fathom why God would let anyone suffer such a disgraceful, lonely and horrific death, let alone His own Son.

But when one meditates on the meaning of the Cross through Sacred Scripture they can see a beauty and power which includes the answer to their own personal suffering. They can see an antidote as it were to their own pain, anger, bitterness and lack of forgiveness in their life.

Through the Cross, God the Father answers the why of suffering. The Cross is the response to Adam and Eve in the beginning seeking to usurp God's power, and thus have no one telling them what to do. Therefore their sin was against an eternal being and was eternal. It could only be atoned for by someone who could represent humanity as well as representing God. So God sent His only Son to become one of us. The second person of the Trinity took on human nature and retained His own divine nature. Therefore He was fully God and fully human. His greatest sacrifice was giving His all, His own life for all of humanity; He could represent humanity as well as God and thus atone for the eternal sin.

As I shared above God understands suffering. He can identify with us because He has walked in our shoes so to speak. Jesus suffered rejection as well as humiliation. He had His clothes taken from Him, leaving Him naked as well as vulnerable. His punishment for loving the outcasts and for revealing Himself as equal to God was crucifixion which was reserved for criminals. Jesus thus suffered the humiliation of being a heavenly king but was sentenced to torture whereby His skin was ripped from His flesh and He suffered death on the tree. How ironic that Adam and Eve's sin was because of a tree and Jesus was crucified on the wood of a tree.

Jesus understands because He suffered an excruciating agony which was more than most of us could endure. Jesus understands because He was taunted by His persecutors and felt abandoned by God as our sins — past and future sins of all humanity separated Him spiritually from the Father.

Pope Francis says: "The joy of the gospel fills the hearts of all those who encounter Jesus." How are you encountering Jesus? Are you encountering Him through spending time in prayer? How about encountering Him through spending time in adoration of the Blessed Sacrament? Are you encountering Him through reading Sacred Scripture? Are you encountering Him through your friends?

These are all ways that we can encounter Jesus. We can encounter Him through His living word, Sacred Scripture; His living Church; through friends; through nature; through prayer, especially in adoration of the Blessed Sacrament; and we can encounter Him through the Sacraments. We encounter His saving and forgiving grace through the Sacrament of Reconciliation.

JUMP into God's ocean of mercy & grace!

"There is no place for selfishness — and no place for fear! Do not be afraid, then, when love makes demands. Do not be afraid when love requires sacrifice." St John Paul II

Notes

1. See Francis, Joy of the Gospel n.6.
2. John Paul II, Salvifici Doloris, Apostolic Letter, n.12.
3. Ibid., n. 13.

Chapter 14

THE THRILL OF THE CHASE

"So you want to be a man? Then trust in me and treat my princesses with pure love. If you seek after me and have a pure heart you will see me. Your friendships will be wholesome and you will open yourself to endless possibilities. With a pure heart you allow me to give you the right princess. Do not strive for love, but love me first. I seek your love most of all. Only then can you truly love anyone, friend or your heart's desire."

From God's love letter.

Once you have pursued God and surrendered all you are to Him you can focus on pursuing a princess of God.

Remember men that each princess is a child of God with a dignity given to her by God. You are called to cherish that dignity and preserve it. Her purity, even if a spiritual virgin or a physical virgin is integral to her dignity. So brothers protect her purity, value it and do not violate it.

Each princess is God's daughter; they are daughters of the heavenly King. Therefore you are answerable to the king in relation to how you treat His princesses. St Paul says:

> For this is the will of God, your sanctification: that you abstain from fornication [sex outside the covenant of marriage]; that each one of you knows how to control your own body in holiness and honor, not with lustful passion, like the Gentiles who do not know God; that no one wrongs or exploits a brother or sister in this matter, because the Lord is an avenger in all these things, just as we have already told you beforehand and solemnly warned you. For God did not call us to impurity but in holiness. Therefore whoever rejects this rejects not human authority but God, who also gives his Holy Spirit to you. (1 Thessalonians 4:4-8)

So treat His daughters with honor, respect and His love. Likewise princesses value, respect and love the princes in your life. They receive their dignity by being sons of God Almighty. They are princes and if you mistreat them or violate their purity you will be answerable to Him.

If you have stumbled in the area of purity, no matter what, you can run to the Sacrament of Reconciliation (Confession) and seek the Lord's forgiveness. He is waiting for you there.

God loves you forever! There is nothing that you can do that will stop God loving you.

There is a thrill in the chase of a princess, especially when they respond and your heart rejoices as the friendship deepens. Brothers, pursue a princess with patience, integrity and respect; and treat each princess in your life as your close friend. For the sister you would like to pursue or are pursuing surrender her to God and allow Him to surprise you. Say to the Lord, "Not my will, but yours be done Lord." God knows you through and through so remember to keep your pursuit centered in prayer. Remember to seek God's will above all else.

If like my chapter on having my heart shattered your pursuit ends in disaster, thank God for the experience and learn from it. Surrender your hurt and your desire to the Lord. Let Him transform your heart and thus your life. In your pursuit seek to live the virtues.

PRINCESSES, IF A PRINCE IS SEEKING YOU

Princesses please do not hide your feelings from the prince pursuing you. It's hard enough for us men to pluck up the courage and to put our heart in the open only to be stabbed or stamped on by your stilettos if you reject us.

Honor your brothers who show interest in you. One way to give us brothers a clue that you like us, without appearing to be overly interested is to tell us that you enjoy our company and want to spend more time with us.

Give the prince who approaches you a chance even if it is only as a friend. For a friend is indeed a great blessing.

Brothers ask God for patience especially if the princess tells you she is "busy". That's what I feel God is telling me at this present time when it comes to pursuing a particular woman after having one date with her at the largest Mass ever held in the Philippines where 6-7 million people were present — it was a Mass presided by Pope Francis.

This pursuit included waiting in a queue for over 5 hours and then being squashed in a crowd of over-eager Catholics where I was left gasping for breath and was so relieved when we reached the front of the queue and entered UST. But it was really worth it. I would eagerly do it again in order to spend more time with her.

Men, regarding the princess whom you are pursuing, if you are led by God then all your sacrifices are worth it.

But even being rejected or having your heart broken gives you the opportunity to draw even nearer to God, to rest in His healing love and abandon all to Him. He wants your pain so that you can move on and so that He can abundantly bless you, especially with His joy.

I know having patience hurts. It's like the movie where Brock is carrying another player on his back across the whole pitch of an American Football field. He yells out, "It hurts!" It hurts more when we don't surrender to Christ. When we hold back it's as if we carry Christ on our backs or even a load of people. But when we surrender and trust in the Lord it is Christ who carries us on His back. He says in Sacred Scripture: "My yoke is easy and my burden is light (Matthew 11:30)."

Trusting God is like being a passenger in a plane. You put your trust in the pilot as the engine's thrust, vibrating the plane and you find your back pressed hard against your seat and you launch into the air. Gazing out the window you see the land falling away. You also trust the pilot as you continue the journey, including through severe turbulence and you keep trusting until you safely land and reach your destination.

Just like flying, trusting in God should be for the entire journey. Yes it can be very scary, especially through the turbulences of life and also especially if you are used to controlling things your way. So it takes faith to let go of your inhibitions and fears, and trust in your loving God. He has the best in store for you. Yes trusting in God can also hurt. Sometimes God asks us to change our ways and it can really hurt. If we are in a wrong relationship it can be very painful to end it. If we need to change the way we are doing things in an intimate relationship it can also really hurt, especially if one's partner does not understand.

But trusting in God is the best step to take. It leads to true freedom, instead of being held captive by vices. True freedom is being who God called you to be. St Irenaeus says "the glory of God is man fully alive." When one is truly free they are truly alive.

God will not give you any more than you can handle. So He won't bring you a really tough situation where He is not offering you the grace needed to get through that situation. He will always give you the grace to endure (See 1 Corinthians 10:13). You just have to trust in God's loving and generous nature.

Chapter 15
FEAR NOT FOR GOD EQUIPS AND SENDS YOU

Sacred Scripture tells us often to "Be not afraid" or "Fear not". But how can we overcome fear? <u>Courage is not the absence of fear but the embracing and overcoming of one's fear.</u> Courage is thus a decision to overcome the doubts of oneself and others and also the taunts of others. Jesus showed us true courage. That courage meant submitting to God the Father's will and embracing His fear at all cost. Jesus paid the greatest cost, brutal torture and murder.

What is God telling you not to be afraid of? Do you have a fear of losing loved ones or a fear of the future? Maybe you have a fear of getting close to people because in the past you lost them when they betrayed you or moved to another city. Just like the previous chapter God wants your all. He wants you to surrender everything to Him.

Now that you have surrendered everything to Jesus, know that you are truly loved by the Blessed Trinity and have your heart transformed by God's grace, especially as you frequent the sacraments, then it is now that you can effectively love others.

This means that from now on you can be happy and content where you are right now. Be thankful for everything that God has given you. Be thankful for your life, your family and your friends. Be thankful that your God is also your closest friend. Yes God is your bestie! He is your bff (best friend forever) because He knows you even better than you know or will ever know yourself on earth.

Jesus says: "Are not five sparrows sold for two pennies? Yet not one of them is forgotten in God's sight. But even the hairs of your head are all counted. Do not be afraid; you are of more value than many sparrows (Luke 12:7)."

If it is God's will, now you are ready, through loving God and self first, and having a grateful heart, to love that special someone God has prepared for you. Or maybe God is still forming one of you or both of you. Maybe God is teaching you something really important such as forming the virtue of patience in you. Your love of God, your relationship with God will cement any God-ordained relationship that He has planned for you.

We are called to know our faith (love it), study it and share it. Because we are blessed we must share our faith with others. Also because we are loved by God we must share our faith. God is calling us to continually be transformed. Like our prized car, we can continually be upgraded. But it's also much different because our transformation is not just added extras, but our transformation is a new heart for God and others. Our transformation is spiritual. It is where we have a new heart for God and we are becoming more like Christ. It is knowing that we are fully united with Christ through the Sacraments, that we respond whole heartedly to Christ. In becoming more like Christ we are becoming more fully human, who we were called to be, images of our wonderful God, Jesus Christ.

God never said that we would not sin. He never said we would not stumble on our journey of faith. Sometimes our walk with the Lord is like climbing an enormous mountain. It's so hard because we can't see the destination but we know that it's ahead of us. If we walk off the path we will put ourselves in danger. We will be in spiritual danger so we must stick to the path at all times, to keep safe.

The path is Christ. Apart from Christ we will not reach our destination. Christ is the way, the truth and the life. He calls us to walk in His ways, to walk His path.

We are also called to bring others to this mountain and to help keep them focused on the path, on Jesus. We are called to be spiritual mountaineers, that through our experience we can help others. We can console them when they are hurt, or are tempted to give up the journey, even for a short time. We are called to urge them on but also when walking with them to show great patience and great love. At times we will also be called to challenge them, even rebuke others but with love.

As spiritual mountaineers or even as soldiers of Christ, we will be wounded. We will be hurt and we will suffer. Even the great saints showed us that they are people who committed mistakes but never gave up. St Peter, like us a disciple of Jesus, was fully committed in mind and heart to follow the Lord, but at his greatest temptation He fell by denying that He even knew the Lord. In effect He was denying that Jesus was His best friend.

How that would have really hurt Jesus and ripped at His heart.

I love the message of this t-shirt:

God calls for great resilience through His grace. He calls for us, like Jesus carrying the Cross, to get up from where we have fallen and to continue the journey. But this time He takes our cross from us and replaces it with a tiny cross. Jesus is the one bearing our load. With His grace the load will indeed become much lighter. Even enabling us to be joyful through our time of great trial or suffering. But this joy will come through surrender and our being grateful with our life and what God is calling us to endure.

God commissions us to go to the whole world. At the end of the book of Matthew Jesus gives what is known as the Great Commission to His disciples and thus to us: "Go therefore into the whole world, proclaiming the good news, baptizing in the name of the Father and the Son and the Holy Spirit. And teaching all that I have commanded you (Matthew 28:19-20)."

God is too sending us into the whole world to proclaim the Good News. We can proclaim through social media, especially sharing inspiring articles or quotes. We can share quotes from Sacred Scripture and also quotes from the saints.

Chapter 16

CONCLUSION

God our Father, calls us to love Him first. He seeks our love above all else. In fact we are to love Him even more than any current girlfriend or future spouse. Our love for God will last for all eternity. So we need to build on that relationship now. We are called to deepen our relationship with Him through reading Sacred Scripture, prayer and partaking in the sacraments.

As part of our adventure with God we are called to surrender every area of our lives to Him. Often we have fears of it being too hard or not being worthy to be loved by God and to love Him in return. But God is calling you to surrender totally so that He can give you even more blessings, including challenges to make you grow as a Christian. Hopefully you have surrendered everything to God, even your fears, so that He can truly work even more powerfully in your life.

He also calls us to have a pure heart. We should change our way of thinking, where the princesses in our lives are treated with respect and not as sexual objects. Jesus said: "You have heard that it was said, 'You shall not commit adultery.' But I say to you that everyone who looks at a woman with lust has already committed adultery with her in his heart (Matthew 5:27-28)."

Therefore just looking, with lust, is not ok. In having a pure heart we will be more open to seeing God and hearing Him speak to us in our everyday lives.

Often as men we especially forget that we are called to take care of ourselves spiritually. Our calling is to be spiritual athletes and warriors. We need to take care of our physical bodies as well as our spiritual bodies. God thirsts for us. He is calling us to spend more time with Him. Therefore we need to set time aside daily to pray — to listen to Him and to respond, as well as interceding for others. And we need to set time aside daily to read His word as well as study our Catholic faith. I have other books and writings to help you study it.

I am aware that other Christians besides Catholics will be reading these two books. I pray that God will indeed move your heart profoundly. For those who have left the Catholic Church it is sad that you did not find the fullness of life within the Church. Please remember that the door is always open in all Catholic Churches and adoration chapels for you to visit or even return wholeheartedly.

As you have read in the chapter "Transformation to Greatness" it is never too late to be transformed into the living image of Jesus Christ. We are called to constantly seek after holiness, which is being His image. We may have been broken inside but God wants to completely heal us. It's vital to talk about our hurts, to an expert, such as a priest or pastor; and it's vital to confess our sins in the Sacrament of Reconciliation if we are Catholic. God is waiting there to give us graces to strengthen us and to make us more like His Son, Jesus Christ.

Real men do go to church. In doing so they can receive the self-gift of Jesus Christ through the Holy Eucharist. They can thus have an intimate uniting with Jesus when He gives Himself totally to us, freely and unreservedly — He gives us His Body, Blood, Soul and Divinity. So as St Peter tells us we thus share in Christ's divinity. That's why John 6:54 says those who eat His Body and drink His Blood have eternal life.

God also calls us to never forget the poor, but to truly love them. We are called to be generous with our resources. St John Chrysostom says re the poor: "Not to share one's wealth with the poor is to steal from them and to take away their livelihood. It is not our own goods which we hold, but theirs".

These words truly strike the heart. How can we not be moved by them, moved to action?

When we seek the love of God in our lives above everything else, we are opening ourselves to God's wonderful plan for us. Any relationship which is open to leading to marriage should be centered on Christ if it is to be the strongest marriage.

In order to be truly a man, we are called not to reduce our lives to that of sexual gratification but to seek to be transformed into the image of Christ.

God calls us not to strive for love but to love Him with all our heart, mind and soul first and our neighbor as ourself. Once we have pursued God then we can discern pursuing a princess of God. Each princess is a child of God with a dignity given to her by God. You are called to cherish that dignity and preserve it. Her purity, even if a spiritual virgin or a physical virgin is integral to her dignity. So brothers protect her purity, value it and do not violate it.

Our adventure with God is indeed like climbing a mountain. It is bloody hard at times, but know this, that if you trust God totally and follow His commands, loving Him totally, He promises you a safe arrival at the summit, heaven.

Author's Note

Worth the Chase is my fifth book and my first co-authored project. Other titles I have written are: Set Free!; Born to be Free; God: Fact or Fiction? and Crusades Rediscovered. I have a Bachelor of Theology degree. On the personal front I am currently a leader in CFC Singles for Christ.

I am seeking to have this book translated. I would dearly love that to include Portuguese and Spanish. Your prayers for this endeavor and any other assistance you could give would be greatly appreciated.

At the time of writing Elly and I are preparing to launch this book in the Philippines. I have been to this beautiful country twice. The presentations I have given here include The New Evangelization; Theology of the Body; Crusades; and Life and Joy through the Holy Eucharist. It was truly a wonderful time of empowering others to love and share their faith. Video clips can be viewed on my Youtube channel.

Please consider blessing my mission financially and inspiring others by purchasing copies of my books for your local library, parish or Church.

Feel free to add me in Facebook as well as viewing my material via:

> www.facebook.com/godfactauthor
> www.facebook.com/godisfact
> www.youtube.com/kiwiauthor
> www.facebook.com/groups/catholicbigmag
> www.godfactauthor.hubpages.com
> www.godfact.com

I have a best friend who is the editor of an on-line Catholic Magazine called Catholic Bigmag. It contains inspirational articles, testimonies and down to earth writing from everyday lay Catholics, as well as priests and nuns. Please email me for further details how to get your free copy of all three issues in PDF format. The chapter, "Transformation to Greatness" was an adaptation of an article I wrote for the magazine.

For speaking engagements please email me on brendanr@ihug.co.nz. I will gladly send you my speaking engagements brochure.

If you want to be kept informed of upcoming books by myself and also a sequel to this book, then please email me: brendanr@ihug.co.nz.

Please consider purchasing copies of my six eBooks on www.amazon.com as well as other eBook sites. Email me and I can send you links to the books.

Yours in Christ

God bless

Brendan Roberts

WWW.AMAZON.COM/DP/B00B0H3AMM

God: Fact or Fiction? is where science, theology and faith come alive. Read the first chapter for free on your PC or mobile phone on www.amazon.com. Encounter fascinating subjects of the universe as well heroics of faith, culminating in the great miracle of the Eucharist.

If you were inspired by *Worth Chasing* then go even deeper and let your faith sparkle through Crusades Rediscovered when reading more about being chaste and Theology of the Body in Crusades Rediscovered as we are to live our lives as self-gift. Also read about God's divine mercy and have the book of Genesis come alive like never before!

POCKET BOOKLET ON THE HOLY EUCHARIST & CHURCH.

Learn about the Real Presence of Christ in the Eucharist and why Catholics treasure this wonderful sacrament so much. Quotes from Sacred Scripture and the Church Fathers will amaze you.

GOD IS FACT FACEBOOK GROUP

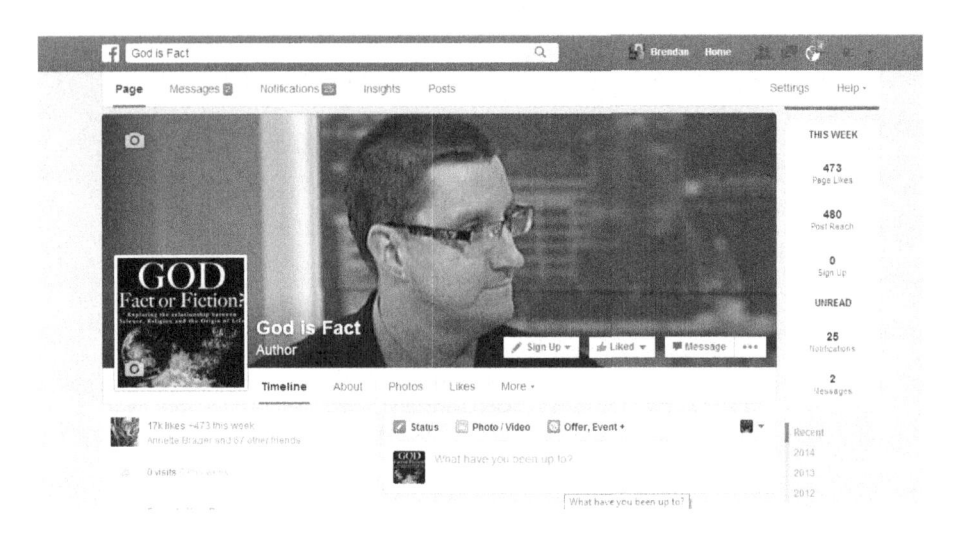

To join God is Fact Facebook Group either type in God is Fact in Facebook search or go to facebook.com/godfact.

WORTH THE CHASE FACEBOOK GROUP

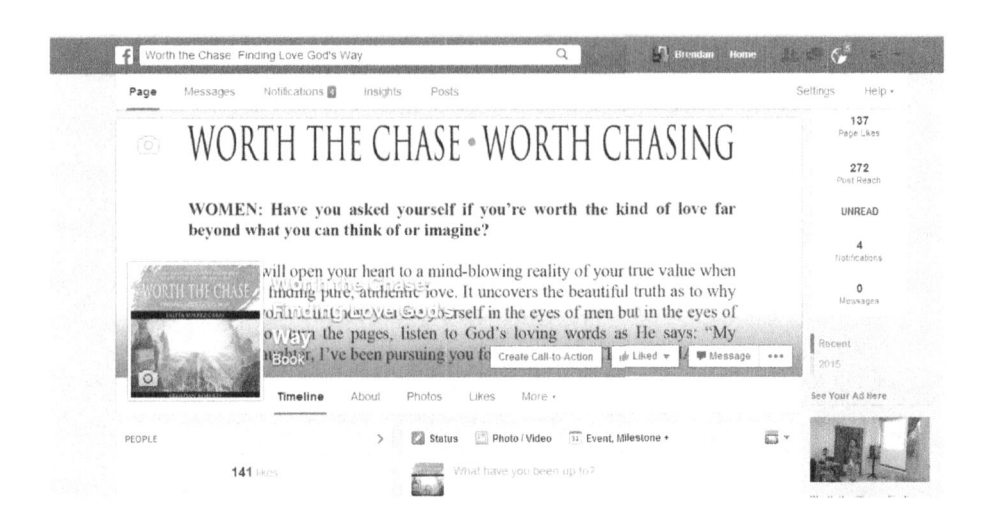

To join Worth the Chase Facebook Group either type in Worth the Chase in Facebook search or go to facebook.com/worthchase.

Last Message From The Authors

We are very excited about this book! Both Elly and I firmly believe that God is the author of *Worth the Chase* and *Worth Chasing*. We honor our loving God, Jesus Christ because He is the one who made our paths cross. He is the one who gave Elly the concept for the books. We do not claim the credit. But we want to give Jesus our heartfelt thanks for choosing us.

It has been an amazing journey which has seen both of us changing as we were challenged writing this book. These great challenges include after completing the editing a draft of the book I lost the entire file when my computer crashed. I also had to reformat the whole book. Writing books over the years I have experienced big computer or software problems often when nearing completion of each book. With *Worth the Chase* there were also personal challenges that came our way too.

But writing this book was really worth it. So worth it we plan to write a sequel.

We are delighted that this book and Brendan's other titles are available in St Paul's Bookstore, Daughters of St Paul Bookstore and soon National Bookstore in the Philippines.

When it comes to promotion, we need you! If you can find the time to share our posts from our Facebook Groups that will be greatly appreciated. But even more importantly if this book has touched your heart, and inspired you to draw closer to our wonderful God then email us. You can email Elly and Brendan at worththechase2@gmail.com. You our readers are in our prayers. May God bless you abundantly.

Made in the USA
Columbia, SC
05 November 2020